ACKNOWLEDG

In any life endeavor the results of our efforts are merely a reflection of those that have positively impacted our lives. I thank all those who, by my simply knowing you, have contributed to the mosaic of my thoughts, ideas, and existence.

Specifically, I acknowledge my loving wife for her consistent support, my friend and partner Donald Bodenbach for incorporating in me the belief of possibility, Mr. Scott Satren and Mr. Richard Monast for defining friendship, the Barlean family for providing me with the vehicle to get to where I want to go, the brilliant insight of Dr. Michael Murray and Miss Ann Louise Gittleman for providing me with the initial impetus to look further into the important issue of essential fatty acid nutrition, and my friends and family for their positive influence on my life.

OTHER SUGGESTED READING
Available from Progressive Health Publishing
Understanding Fats & Oils, by M. Murray & J. Beutler
Fats That Can Save Your Life, by R. Erdmann, Ph.D.

Copyright © Jade Beutler 1996

Cover design: John Odam Design Associates
Cover photography: Werner Kalber, Professional Photographic Services
Layout: Kristi Paulson Mendola
Editing: JoAnn Koppany

Library of Congress Catalog Card Number: 96-067523
ISBN 0-9645075-2-8

Flax for Life! is meant for education purposes only. It is not intended as medical advice. The authors and publisher recommend consulting a qualified health care professional for any condition requiring medical advice, diagnosis, or prescription.

PROGRESSIVE HEALTH PUBLISHING
315 First Street #U-198
Encinitas, CA 92024

Praise for *Flax for Life!*

"I have been recommending flax oil to my patients for a number of years. This very helpful book effectively answers the most asked question, how do I take it?"

Dr. Julian Whitaker
Editor, *Health and Healing*
Director, Whitaker Wellness Institute

"Flax for Life! will become a valuable tool in my clinical practice as it provides delicious ways to incorporate the tremendous health benefits of flaxseed oil into the American diet."

Dr. Michael Murray
Author, *Encyclopedia of Natural Medicine*
Editor, *The American Journal of Natural Medicine*

"Jade Beutler has filled a gaping hole in healthy food menus with his book *Flax for Life!* Not only do we get our essential fatty acids from his recipes, but also superb meals. The sauces and breads especially are great."

Dr. Michael Colgan
Director, Colgan Institute
Author, *Optimum Sports Nutrition*
The New Nutrition, Medicine for the Millennium

"The benefits of flax are essential. *Flax for Life!* combines good sense with great taste. Eating well & healthy can truly be the same—here's how."

Dr. Marcus Laux, N.D.
Editor, *Naturally Well*

"This book is an important contribution to the understanding of the critical role fats play in the diet, more specifically flaxseed oil. Jade Beutler has done a remarkable job of making it a simple task of learning how and why we need fats for a healthy diet."

Terry Lemerond
President, Enzymatic Therapy
Radio Host, *Prescription for Health*

"Flax for Life! is a perfect companion to my book *Fats That Can Save Your Life* in that while my book addresses a comprehensive read on the importance of essential fatty acids, Jade Beutler teaches you how to incorporate these lifesaving nutrients into your daily diet with flaxseed oil."

Dr. Robert Erdmann
Director, Medabolics Clinic, Tunbridge Wells, England
Author, *Fats That Can Save Your Life*

"With fat phobia paralyzing America, it's refreshing to see Jade Beutler telling us to eat more 'healthy fats' and oils. Essential fatty acids are vital to our health and flax oil is truly the king! The entire world will greatly benefit from your well-researched flaxseed oil recipe book!"

Jay Robb
President, Jay Robb Enterprises
Author, *The Fat Burning Diet*

Flax for Life!

$\mathscr{F}$lax for Life!

101 DELICIOUS
RECIPES AND TIPS FEATURING
FABULOUS FLAX OIL

....

Jade Beutler, R.R.T, R.C.P

FOREWORD BY
Ann Louise Gittleman, M.S.
Certified Nutrition Specialist

REMARKS BY
Dr. Michael Murray
Dr. Julian Whitaker
Dr. Marcus Laux
Dr. Michael Colgan

PROGRESSIVE
HEALTH
PUBLISHING

315 First Street #U-198
Encinitas, CA 92024

ACKNOWLEDGMENTS

In any life endeavor the results of our efforts are merely a reflection of those that have positively impacted our lives. I thank all those who, by my simply knowing you, have contributed to the mosaic of my thoughts, ideas, and existence.

Specifically, I acknowledge my loving wife for her consistent support, my friend and partner Donald Bodenbach for incorporating in me the belief of possibility, Mr. Scott Satren and Mr. Richard Monast for defining friendship, the Barlean family for providing me with the vehicle to get to where I want to go, the brilliant insight of Dr. Michael Murray and Miss Ann Louise Gittleman for providing me with the initial impetus to look further into the important issue of essential fatty acid nutrition, and my friends and family for their positive influence on my life.

OTHER SUGGESTED READING

Available from Progressive Health Publishing
Understanding Fats & Oils, by M. Murray & J. Beutler
Fats That Can Save Your Life, by R. Erdmann, Ph.D.

Copyright © Jade Beutler 1996

Cover design: John Odam Design Associates
Cover photography: Werner Kalber, Professional Photographic Services
Layout: Kristi Paulson Mendola
Editing: JoAnn Koppany

Library of Congress Catalog Card Number: 96-067523
ISBN 0-9645075-2-8

Flax for Life! is meant for education purposes only. It is not intended as medical advice. The authors and publisher recommend consulting a qualified health care professional for any condition requiring medical advice, diagnosis, or prescription.

PROGRESSIVE
HEALTH
PUBLISHING

315 First Street #U-198
Encinitas, CA 92024

This book, and any possible good that comes from it, I dedicate to my baby daughter Chloe for the joy and hope she instills in me and, as a result, the motivation I find to positively impact our future generations.

Contents

Foreword

The title of this book *Flax for Life!* couldn't be more fitting.

Flax oil has emerged as one of the most healing foods of our time. Jade Beutler has done a truly admirable job in consolidating massive amounts of research material into a simple user-friendly format. And just wait until you taste the recipes from Jade's own kitchen.

In my own practice I have been using and recommending flax oil for several years now. Not only have I seen firsthand its beautifying bene-fits to the skin, hair, and nails, but I have also experienced a certain calmness and mental focus that flax oil imparts. My clients report alle-viation from aches and pains as well as relief from PMS and menopausal discomforts. Others have noticed a reduction in cholesterol and triglyc-eride levels and best, some have lost weight on just 2 tablespoons of flax oil daily without changing anything else in the diet! The reports and anecdotal evidence just continue to keep piling in.

In *Flax for Life!* you'll find a flax recipe for everyone. Because flax is good for the whole family, you'll soon be experimenting on your own. So be sure and peruse the "Flax for Thought" section at the beginning of each chapter which will give you even more delightful tips for flax-ing up your day.

If you are anything like me, you'll start looking for ways to get flax oil into everyday foods. I think my passion for air popped popcorn is just an excuse to indulge in more delicious flax oil because I love to driz-zle it on top.

Now get ready and get set to enjoy the health food discovery of the century!

Ann Louise Gittleman, M.S.
Certified Nutrition Specialist

1

$\mathcal{P}$ut the Fat Back

Put the fat back?

That's right, you read it correctly the first time, "Put the fat back."

I'm sure most of you have heard about good cholesterol and bad cholesterol. Well guess what? The same is true of fat. In fact, the good or right fats and oils help build the HDL "good" cholesterol while the bad or wrong fats contribute to the LDL "bad" cholesterol.

Did you know that the right kinds of fat are actually essential to life itself, and without them we are much more susceptible to disease and death? What if I told you that the right fats, or more specifically what are known as *essential fatty acids,* protect us from the most devastating diseases of our time, including heart disease, cancer, and stroke? Now don't take my word for it, research scientists worldwide are rediscovering the almost unbelievable health-enhancing and therapeutic potential of essential fatty acids.

We must learn how to avoid the unhealthy fats such as excess saturated fats from animal foods and the fats from hydrogenated sources like margarine, shortening, and fried foods. Plus, we need to include the vital essential fatty acids from unrefined vegetable oils in our everyday diet.

And this is what this recipe book is all about, putting the right fat into the diet.

You may be wondering about all the no-fat and low-fat food products lining our grocery store shelves. Let me ask you a question. Have you actually lost any weight since going low fat? If you are like most Americans, probably not. In fact, statistics tell us that since America has been cutting the fat, we have actually gained more weight per capita as a nation.

It shouldn't come as any surprise that many of these no-fat and low-fat products are made up primarily of simple carbohydrates from white sugar and/or white flour. Read any label of those fat-free cookies and you will find sugar and corn syrup heading the ingredient parade. Refined carbohydrates have zero nutritional value but are loaded with calories. When eaten in large quantities, they are converted to fat in the body. We are now being served gigantic portions. For example, muffins have become mammoth and bagels have become oversized since the advent of the fat-free era.

Ironically, the fat you have been trying to avoid can actually aid in weight loss if it is the right kind. The essential fatty acids help to adjust metabolism naturally, increasing the body's ability to burn excess calories. The good fats even go so far as to ferry the bad fats out of our cells and tissues. Since bad fats can harbor toxins, this is terrific news all the way around.

Where can we find these so-called good fats—the essential fatty acids? If you lived approximately 100 years ago, you could have found these healthy fats in raw seeds and nuts as well as in vegetable oils extracted the old-fashioned way. Even meats had higher tissue levels of essential fatty acids 100 years ago because animals were allowed to range free and graze on vegetable matter containing the essential fats. These healing and protective fatty acids used to be prevalent in our diets.

Unfortunately because of modern manufacturing methods and refinement of foods rich in the protective and healing essential fatty acids, these good fats are almost nonexistent in our daily foods. Is it any coincidence that heart disease, cancer, and stroke have become our nation's leading killers since the advent of modern technology for processing foods and oils?

For the first time in almost 100 years, the essential fatty acids are once again becoming available as found in nature's richest source, unrefined flax oil. Thus the title of this book: *Flax for Life!* People across the country are flocking to their local health food stores for a bottle of this liquid gold.

Dramatic evidence suggests that flax oil, and a special plant fiber found in flaxseed called *lignan,* can protect us against heart disease and cancer as well as other degenerative diseases. For nearly 50 years, Dr. Johanna Budwig, a German biochemist and Nobel Prize nominee, has utilized unrefined flax oil in conjunction with an organic diet to fight cancer. Even here in the U.S., numerous research studies have been concluded with flaxseed and cancer, including research by the National Cancer Institute (NCI). The NCI found that flaxseed did indeed have an anticancer effect—even to match some chemotherapeutic drugs—but without the nasty side effects found with the drugs!

Women have become increasingly aware of the rising epidemic of breast cancer. Unfortunately, 1 out of 8 women today will be diagnosed with breast cancer. Is it possible that flax oil could significantly reduce the incidence of this deadly disease? Scientific research on women and breast cancer has established that women who have the highest amount of the omega-3 fatty acid most prevalent in flax oil have the lowest incidence of breast cancer. More important, if any of these women had an existing tumor, those with the highest amount of omega-3 in their breast tissue still had the lowest incidence of the tumor spreading to other tissues and organs.

What about other women's health concerns? The use of flax oil has been found to ease the mood swings and uncomfortable cramping associated with PMS as well as ease the transition of menopause. Also, the essential fatty acids found in flax oil are unsurpassed for building strong nails, lustrous hair, and radiant skin.

If you own a pet, remember to add a teaspoon or two of flax oil to your animal's food. In Europe, flax oil was once widely used to promote beautiful and glistening fur, strong hooves and nails, vibrant eyes, and robust health.

We can all appreciate the added protection against cancer that flax oil can bring, but what about heart disease? Doesn't fat increase one's chances of cardiovascular complications? The answer is yes, and no. Once again we must qualify the type of fat we are talking about. Excessive ingestion of saturated fat and especially "funny fats" (hydrogenated oils) will increase the likelihood of heart disease, but the absolute opposite is true of the essential fats found in flax oil. Flax oil has been found to significantly decrease the possibility of heart disease on many fronts. Flax oil lubricates and relaxes our blood vessels, helps to clear clogged arteries, and acts as a valuable energy source that keeps the heart beating healthy and strong. This is the reason why flax oil is considered so "heart smart."

The good fats found in flax affect our health at nearly every level. They combat infection and allergy by boosting our immune system. They act as cellular batteries, supercharging every one of our one hundred trillion cells, becoming incorporated into their membranes, and capturing photon energy from the sun.

Now, if I called you a "fat head" you would probably be offended. Yet, it just might be the highest compliment I could pay you. The essential fats found in flax have been postulated to improve memory, behavior, and mental ability. Wouldn't you like to see your children pulling higher grades in school? This is exactly what happened in Wisconsin when a local bread baker started including flaxseed in his bakery products and donating them to local elementary schools. The parents and teachers also noted that the children's attendance and behavior had improved.

Research done by a prominent psychologist found that the essential fats improved the psychological conditions of his mentally challenged patients. Athletes have noticed improved performance and decreased muscle fatigue as a result of the fats in flax improving the availability of oxygen to their hardworking muscles. Patients with the deadly disease lupus nephritis have reason for optimism after research showed that flax oil could decrease mortality (death) caused by their disease by over 60 percent!

What about relief from inflammation and arthritis pain? Flax delicately balances hormones in the body that aggravate these conditions. Persons suffering from skin conditions, such as psoriasis and eczema, have also found relief with flax oil supplementation.

I could continue on and on extolling the benefits of flax. The essential good fats have been found to be therapeutic in over 60 diseases and illnesses. The main point I would like you to remember is that you can avoid the majority of these health challenges by following a healthful diet with the inclusion of flax oil. This book is designed to serve as a tool to help you incorporate the highly important essential fatty acids in the form of flax oil into everyday wholesome foods.

Flax oil is quickly becoming one of the most popular health foods in our country. Research scientists continue to learn of its practically unlimited potential in human nutrition. Many leading health and nutrition authorities are recommending flax oil as an integral part of a foundation for a healthy diet. The excitement triggered by flax is truly causing a "fat revolution" away from no fat and low fat to the right fat as found most abundantly in flax.

The growing popularity of flax has not gone unnoticed by food manufacturers wanting to boost the nutritional value of the foods they offer to consumers. While flax does not lend itself to modern manufacturing and refinement, flaxseed has been used successfully in baked goods, and flax oil seems a perfect ingredient for salad dressings. Health-conscious companies are working to make the consumption of flaxseed and flax oil more practical to consumers. It would appear that our 100-year departure from the essential fats has come full circle. The bottom line is that flax is here to stay, and you can expect to hear more about its amazing attributes.

I imagine you are all thinking, "This sounds too good to be true — flax oil sure sounds like a panacea."

Flax oil, along with the essential fatty acids it contains, is just one more example of the truly unbelievable healing power of natural, unrefined foods. In fact, if our food wasn't so heavily refined, we wouldn't be faced with the illnesses that the essential fatty acids and other valuable nutrients so powerfully protect us against.

We also must remember that the essential fatty acids found in flax oil are truly essential to life, and we must get them in our foods in order to appreciate optimal, vibrant health and long life. Is it important to reintroduce these nutrient powerhouses, the essential fatty acids, back into our diet? You bet it is, and you can start right here and right now!

Consider the impact you can have on your health and the health of your loved ones by simply committing to get as little as one tablespoon of unrefined flax oil in your daily diet. What a small price to pay for protection against cancer, heart disease, stroke, and other devastating illnesses. Thousands of folks across the country have been experiencing the profound health effects associated with this remarkable food—not to mention the beautifying effects it can have.

In *Flax For Life!* you are presented with simple and practical ways to incorporate flax oil into your daily diet. You will learn how to easily add this healing and protective food with fun, easy-to-prepare, and delicious snacks, dips, soups, and meals. You can find unrefined, organic, expeller pressed flax oil at most health food stores, usually located in the refrigerator section.

I know you will agree with me that we have been deprived of our essential fatty acids for too long. It's high time to put the fat back, the right fat that is, as found in unrefined flax oil.

Long and vibrant health to you and yours.

Bon appétit!

2

Breakfast and Breads

START YOUR DAY SUPERCHARGED
WITH THE RIGHT FAT FOUND IN FLAX

FLAX FOR THOUGHT Breakfast is considered by many health experts to be the most important meal of the day. We are literally breaking an approximately 12-hour fast from the day before. Breakfast serves to raise, and hopefully sustain, our blood sugar and energy levels until the noon hour. The addition of flaxseed and flax oil to breakfast foods serves several important functions.

- The essential fats in flax are able to help you maintain consistent energy and blood sugar levels throughout the day.

- The addition of flax to children's diets has been discovered to improve learning ability and behavior. What a great head start to your child's school day!

- The ingestion of foods with flax oil causes a feeling of fullness and fulfillment that follows a satisfying meal.

- The essential fatty acids in flax help to decrease the "stickiness" of blood platelets. The morning hours are considered the most dangerous for risk of heart attack because of sluggish blood flow caused by sticky blood platelets.

Breakfast lends itself well to the addition of flax oil. Here are a few quick and easy ways to improvise with flax at breakfast time.

- Combine one part chilled flax oil with one part melted butter, then chill. The new spread will resemble the consistency of margarine — without all the toxic funny fats and with the addition of the vital essential fatty acids. Use this spread on toast, on baked potatoes, or for any other low-heat application where you would ordinarily use butter or margarine.

- Combine one part flax oil with one part pure maple syrup. You will now have a buttery-tasting maple syrup topping for waffles, French toast, and pancakes. It's a terrific way to sneak the essential fatty acids into your child's diet.

- For a quick, easy, and healthy breakfast, simply stir one tablespoon of flax oil into yogurt and top with your favorite fruit.

- Mix flax oil with your favorite hot cereal for a buttery consistency and nutty flavor.

- For recipes that call for ground flaxseed, simply place whole flaxseed in a coffee grinder and grind until desired consistency is achieved.

Granola-Like Breakfast

4 tablespoons sesame seeds
4 tablespoons sunflower seeds
4 tablespoons flaxseed
4 cups rolled oats
1/4 cup fresh apple juice
cinnamon to taste
1 cup fresh fruit
plain nonfat yogurt to top

- Grind the sesame seeds, sunflower seeds, and flaxseed in a coffee grinder.
- Combine the seed mixture with the oats. Divide into 2 equal portions.
- Soak one portion with the apple juice.
- Place both portions in the refrigerator overnight.
- Stir the portions together. Add the cinnamon and fresh fruit.
- Top with yogurt.

SERVES 4

Fresh Fruit Breakfast Muesli

Flax meal muesli

2 tablespoons flaxseed
1 tablespoon raw honey

- Grind the flaxseed to a coarse consistency in a coffee grinder.
- Place in a serving dish. Add the honey. Combine by thoroughly mashing with a fork.

Yogurt filling

4 ounces plain or vanilla nonfat yogurt
3 tablespoons Barlean's organic flax oil
1 teaspoon raw honey

- Combine all ingredients in a small mixing bowl. Whisk or hand blend to an even consistency.
- Pour over the flax meal muesli.

Toppings

banana slices	cherries	peach slices	peanuts
blackberries	currants	pear slices	pecans
blueberries	fruit juice	cinnamon	pine nuts
raspberries	grapes	ginger	slivered almonds
strawberries	grated apple	nutmeg	walnuts

- Top the muesli with the toppings of your choice.

SERVES 2

Banana, Apple, and Date Breakfast Pudding
A breakfast or anytime treat, tasty and chewy.

3 large dates, pits removed
1 apple, diced
1 large frozen banana
3 sections of an orange
1 1/2 tablespoons Barlean's organic flax oil
yogurt and walnuts to top (optional)

- Place all ingredients in a blender or food processor and process to desired consistency.
- Serve in a bowl or a tall glass.
- Top with yogurt and walnuts if desired.

SERVES 1 TO 2

Apple Muesli

*Popularized in Europe, muesli is a tremendously healthy way
to start your day.*

2 tablespoons oatmeal
4 teaspoons water
2 apples
2 1/2 tablespoons wheat germ
juice of 1/2 lemon
3/4 cup yogurt
1 tablespoon raisins
2 tablespoons Barlean's organic flax oil
2 tablespoons raw honey
3 tablespoons chopped walnuts

- Soak the oatmeal overnight in the water.
- Grate the apple or process in a food processor.
- Combine all ingredients and mix well. Eat immediately.

SERVES 2

Fruit Lupes

A delicious fruit cereal the way Mother Nature intended.

2 large crisp apples, cored
1 tablespoon currants
1/4 cup shredded coconut
1/4 cup diced dried figs
1/4 cup coarsely ground almonds
1/2 teaspoon cinnamon
1/4 cup apple juice
2 teaspoons pure maple syrup
2 teaspoons Barlean's organic flax oil

- Place the apples and currants in a food processor and coarsely grind.
- Combine the apple mixture with the coconut, figs, almonds, cinnamon, and apple juice.
- In a small bowl or cup, thoroughly blend the maple syrup and flax oil.
- Add the flax-maple syrup mixture to the other ingredients. Mix well and serve.

SERVES 2

Hot Carob Cereal
A rich and warming cereal.

2 1/4 cups water or rice milk
1 cup oatmeal
1 tablespoon unsweetened carob powder
1/2 teaspoon cinnamon
2 tablespoons Barlean's organic flax oil
1 tablespoon raisins
2 teaspoons raw honey
plain nonfat yogurt to top (optional)

- Bring the water or rice milk to a boil. Stir in the oatmeal, carob powder, and cinnamon. Cook for 3 minutes.
- Remove from heat and stir in the flax oil, raisins, and honey. Let sit with lid on for 1 minute.
- Serve topped with yogurt if desired.

SERVES 2

Happy Apple Breakfast
Other rolled grains such as wheat, barley, rye, or triticale can be used in various combinations instead of some or all of the rolled oats. All of these grains have the same cooking characteristics.

1 1/2 cups rolled oats
2 1/2 cups water, milk, or apple juice
1 medium green or golden apple, sliced
1/4 cup currants, raisins, or chopped dates
1/4 cup freshly roasted pumpkin seeds (optional)
2 tablespoons Barlean's organic flax oil
raw honey to sweeten
plain nonfat yogurt to top (optional)

- Combine all ingredients, except the flax oil and honey, in a saucepan. Simmer on the stove for 10 minutes. Cover and let sit for 5 minutes.
- Stir in the flax oil and honey to taste.
- Serve topped with yogurt if desired.

SERVES 2

Buttery Banana Pancakes

The illusion of buttery-rich pancakes made easy by combining maple syrup with flax oil.

Syrup

1/4 cup pure maple syrup
1/4 cup Barlean's organic flax oil

Pancakes

1 1/2 cups whole wheat pastry flour
1/4 teaspoon salt or salt substitute
3 teaspoons baking powder
1 3/4 cups rice milk, soy milk, or nonfat milk
1 tablespoon butter or extra virgin olive oil
1 1/2 ripe bananas, sliced

- Whisk the maple syrup together with the flax oil until thoroughly blended.
- Combine the flour, salt, and baking powder. Sift into a mixing bowl.
- Pour the milk into the flour mixture and mix until thoroughly combined.
- Lightly butter or oil a griddle and preheat to medium heat.
- Pour 1/4 cup of the batter at a time onto the griddle. Add the banana slices randomly to the top of the pancake. Cook about 3 minutes until the bottom is lightly browned. Turn over and cook until the second side is lightly browned.
- Serve at once. Top liberally with flax-maple syrup.

SERVES 2 TO 3

Barlean Butter

At last, a spreadable alternative to margarine with half the saturated fat of butter. Use on toast, bagels, or muffins.

1 stick of butter
4 ounces Barlean's organic flax oil

- Cut the butter into cubes and gently melt in a small saucepan.
- Pour the liquefied butter into a small, sealable container.
- Stir in the flax oil. Seal and set in the refrigerator to solidify.

French Toast with Flax-Maple Syrup

French toast with a buttery-like maple syrup made by adding flax oil.

Syrup
1/4 cup pure maple syrup
1/4 cup Barlean's organic flax oil

French toast
1/2 cup whole wheat pastry flour
1/4 teaspoon salt or salt substitute
1 cup rice milk or soy milk
6 slices whole-grain bread
cinnamon and nutmeg to taste

- Whisk the maple syrup together with the flax oil until thoroughly blended.
- Mix the flour and salt in a bowl large enough to accommodate one piece of toast. Aerate the mixture with a wire whisk.
- Pour the milk into the center of the flour and mix briskly.
- Let the batter sit for 20 minutes.
- Heat a lightly buttered griddle. Mix the batter well. Dip each slice of bread in batter to coat completely. Cook about 3 minutes until the first side is lightly browned, then turn over and cook the second side.
- Sprinkle with cinnamon and nutmeg to taste.
- Top French toast with flax-maple syrup.

SERVES 2 TO 3

Vanilla-Raisin Cream of Rice
A hot and healthy rice cereal.

1 cup organic brown rice
3 1/2 cups water, soy milk, rice milk, or milk
1/2 cup raisins
2 teaspoons vanilla extract
4 tablespoons Barlean's organic flax oil
plain nonfat yogurt to top

- Finely grind the rice to a powdery consistency in a blender, coffee grinder, or nut/seed grinder.
- Bring the water or milk to a boil in a large pot. Whisk in the rice powder. Add the raisins. Cover and simmer for 15 minutes.
- Remove from heat. Stir in the vanilla and flax oil.
- Serve immediately.
- Top with yogurt to complete the oil/protein combination.

SERVES 3 TO 4

Barlean's Best Oatmeal
A delicious, nutty-flavored hot breakfast cereal. An incredibly healthy way to start a new day.

1 cup oat groats (whole oat grain)
4 cups rice milk, soy milk, milk, or water
1/2 cup raisins
1/2 teaspoon vanilla
dash of cinnamon
raw honey to flavor
4 tablespoons Barlean's organic flax oil
plain nonfat yogurt to top

- Grind the oat groats in a blender or coffee grinder to desired consistency (depending on your preference for coarse or fine cereal).
- Bring the milk or water to a rolling boil. Whisk the ground oats into the milk. Add the raisins. Reduce heat and simmer for 20 minutes.
- Remove from heat. Add the vanilla, cinnamon, and honey. Stir in the flax oil.
- Serve topped with yogurt.

SERVES 4

Barlean's Quick and Easy Oatmeal
A quick and simple version of Barlean's Best Oatmeal.

1 cup quick oats
2 cups rice milk, soy milk, milk, or water
1/4 cup raisins
1/4 teaspoon vanilla
dash of cinnamon
raw honey to flavor
2 tablespoons Barlean's organic flax oil
plain nonfat yogurt to top

- Combine the oats, milk, and raisins in a saucepan.
- Bring to a boil. Cook about 1 minute over medium heat, stirring occasionally.
- Remove from heat. Add the vanilla, cinnamon, and honey. Stir in the flax oil.
- Serve topped with yogurt.

SERVES 2 TO 3

Quick Bread

2 cups ground flaxseed*
1 cup whole wheat flour
1 cup all-purpose flour
1 teaspoon salt
2 teaspoons baking soda
4 egg whites or 2 eggs
grated peel from 2 lemons (save lemons for juice)
1/2 cup raw honey or sugar
2 cups raisins, chopped prunes or dates (soak ahead a few minutes; drain)
express lemons for juice, adding enough buttermilk to yield 1 1/2 cups liquid

- * Grind whole flaxseed to the consistency of flour in a coffee grinder.
- Combine ingredients in descending order and mix thoroughly.
- Bake in 6 lightly buttered, small loaf pans (approximately 3" x 7") for 40 minutes at 325°F.

MAKES 6 SMALL LOAVES

Wheat-Free Flax Bread
A recipe for people on a wheat-free diet.

1/2 cup beaten mashed potatoes (or 2 tablespoons dry instant mashed potatoes)

1/4 cup butter

1/4 cup sugar

1/2 cup cooked white rice

6 eggs, separated

1 1/2 cups brown rice flour

2 tablespoons soy flour

3 teaspoons baking powder

1 teaspoon baking soda

1 teaspoon cream of tartar

1/2 teaspoon salt

1/8 teaspoon black pepper (optional)

3/4 cup milk (if using instant potatoes add another 1/2 cup milk)

1/4 cup flaxseed

- If using instant mashed potatoes, reconstitute with the additional 1/2 cup milk.

- Be sure that the potatoes are free of lumps. Cream the potatoes thoroughly with the butter and sugar. Mix in the white rice, then add the egg yolks one at a time, beating thoroughly after each one.

- Sift the dry ingredients together and add to the potato mixture alternately with the milk.

- Beat the egg whites to hold their shape in soft (not stiff) peaks. Fold in the egg whites. Fold in the flaxseed. Pour the batter into 2 lightly buttered 9 1/2" x 5" loaf pans. Bake at 350°F for about 1 hour.

MAKES 2 LOAVES

Whole-Grain Flax Bread

1¼ cups ground flaxseed*
5 cups warm water
4 tablespoons softened raw honey
2½ tablespoons instant yeast
1 cup oatmeal
4 cups unbleached white flour
½ cup whey powder
2 teaspoons salt
8 cups stone-ground whole wheat flour (approximately)

* Grind whole flaxseed to a fine consistency in a coffee grinder.

• Combine the water, honey, and yeast. Let sit for 3 to 4 minutes.

• In a separate bowl, mix the oatmeal, unbleached flour, ground flaxseed, whey powder, and salt. Add these dry ingredients to the yeast mixture and mix well.

• Beat for 5 minutes by hand, then add the whole wheat flour and mix until dough is quite stiff. (If using a bread kneading machine, add the whole wheat flour and mix on high speed for 5 minutes.) Knead. Let rise 15 minutes. Punch down and let rise another 15 minutes. Punch down and shape into loaves.

• Let the bread rise until doubled in size. Bake loaves at 350°F for 40 to 45 minutes.

MAKES 2 LOAVES

Flax Bagels

1/2 cup ground flaxseed*
2 1/4 cups flour
1 teaspoon salt
1 package yeast
2 1/4 cups water (110°F to 130°F)
additional flour for kneading
1/4 cup sugar

* Grind whole flaxseed to the consistency of flour in a coffee grinder.

- Using an electric mixer on low speed for 1 minute, mix the flour, ground flaxseed, salt, yeast, and water. Scrape the bowl, then mix on high speed for 2 to 3 minutes. Add additional flour as needed.

- Place the dough on a floured surface. Knead, adding flour as necessary to form a stiff dough that is smooth and pliable. Place in a greased bowl and cover with a damp, warm towel. Let sit in a warm spot for 10 minutes.

- Working quickly, divide the dough into 12 pieces. Roll each into a ball and punch a hole in the center of the ball with a floured finger.

- Pull the dough gently to form a 2-inch circle. Place on a greased baking sheet. Let rise for 30 to 45 minutes.

- While the dough is rising, bring 6 cups of water to a boil in a large skillet or Dutch oven. Add the sugar. Reduce heat so the water is at a simmer.

- After the bagels have risen, place in the simmering water for 5 minutes, turning once. Remove and place on a wire rack for 3 to 5 minutes.

- Place on a baking sheet and bake in a preheated oven at 375°F for 25 to 30 minutes. When done the bagels should be a golden color.

- If desired, garlic, onion, sesame seeds, herbs, spices, or other flavors may be added to the dry ingredients. Use approximately 1 to 1 1/2 teaspoons of flavor. Sprinkle seeds on bagels after boiling and prior to baking if a topping is desired.

MAKES 12 BAGELS

Flax and Potato Bread

1/4 cup flaxseed
3/4 cup water
1 1/2 cups flour
hot water (approximately 130°F)
2 tablespoons potato flakes
3 tablespoons raw honey
1 tablespoon nonfat milk powder
1 package instant yeast
1 teaspoon salt
1 teaspoon butter
additional flour for kneading

- In a large mixing bowl, soak the flaxseed in warm water for 45 minutes, then add the remaining ingredients.
- Mix with an electric mixer for 1/2 minute. Scrape the bowl and mix on high speed for another 2 to 3 minutes.
- While mixing with a spoon, add additional flour to make a dough you can work by hand.
- Place the dough on a floured surface and knead by hand. Add additional flour to make a stiff, pliable dough.
- Place the dough in a greased bowl. Cover and set aside in a warm spot for 20 minutes.
- Divide the dough into 2 equal pieces. Place in lightly buttered 4 1/4" x 8 1/4" bread pans.
- Set in a warm place with no cool draft until doubled in size.
- Bake at 380°F for 25 minutes or until the crust is a golden color.

MAKES 2 LOAVES

Multigrain Bread

1/2 cup ground flaxseed*
2 cups whole wheat flour
1/2 cup rye flour
1/2 cup oat bran (optional)
4 1/2 cups high-gluten bread flour
1/4 cup sugar
1/4 cup molasses
1/4 cup unrefined canola oil
1 tablespoon dry yeast
2 1/4 cups warm water

* Grind whole flaxseed to the consistency of fine flour in a coffee grinder.
• Combine ingredients in descending order and mix thoroughly.
• Pour dough into 3 standard-size, lightly buttered bread pans.
• Bake at 375°F for about 1 hour or until loaves are loose in pans.

MAKES 3 LOAVES

$\mathscr{D}$ips and Dressings

A QUICK, EASY, AND PRACTICAL WAY
TO GET YOUR DAILY DOSE OF ESSENTIAL FATTY ACIDS

FLAX FOR THOUGHT Dips and salad dressings can harbor many hidden sources of unnatural and dangerous fats and oils in our diet. But, on the other hand, they can become some of our strongest allies in bringing the right fats, the essential fatty acids, back into our diets if they are made with flax oil. Until dips and salad dressings are made available with unrefined flax and vegetable oils, we should fashion our own blends with the recipes found in this chapter.

Here are a couple of tips regarding dips and dressings.

- To ensure healthful salad dressings when dining out, take along your homemade blend in a tightly sealed plastic container.

- After making your dips and salad dressings from healthful oils, be sure to refrigerate them to extend shelf life.

Flax-Almond Mayonnaise
A rich, creamy, and tasty alternative to mayonnaise made with processed oils. Use whenever mayonnaise is called for.

1/4 cup raw almonds
1/4 cup water, soy milk, or rice milk
1/2 teaspoon nutritional yeast
1/4 teaspoon garlic powder
1/4 teaspoon salt or salt substitute
1/4 cup Barlean's organic flax oil
1/4 cup extra virgin olive oil
2 tablespoons lemon juice
1/4 teaspoon apple cider vinegar

- Combine ingredients in a blender or food processor in descending order. Blend on high speed until thick and creamy.
- Refrigerate until ready to use. Keeps 10 days to 2 weeks refrigerated.

MAKES 1 CUP

Fresh Mexican Salsa
A zesty traditional Mexican salsa made even better with the addition of flax oil. Great as a dip for tortilla chips or as a sauce on enchiladas, burritos, and tacos.

3 tomatoes, diced
4 sprigs fresh cilantro
1/2 medium onion, diced
1 scallion, chopped
1 small jalapeño pepper
1/2 cup tomato sauce
3 tablespoons Barlean's organic flax oil

- Combine the tomatoes, cilantro, onion, scallion, and jalapeño pepper in a blender or food processor and process to desired consistency, chunky or saucy.
- In a separate bowl, combine the tomato sauce and flax oil. Stir to a uniform consistency.
- Mix everything together and chill until ready to serve.

MAKES 2 CUPS

Bean Dip

Serve this dip with tortilla chips or firm vegetables,
such as celery, carrots, and bell peppers.

1 16-ounce can or 2 cups cooked cannellini beans (white kidney
    beans), drained and rinsed
4 large cloves garlic, boiled for 5 minutes, then peeled and sliced
2 tablespoons Barlean's organic flax oil
1/4 to 1/2 teaspoon hot pepper sauce
1 to 2 teaspoons minced jalapeño pepper (fresh or canned)

- Combine all ingredients in a food processor and blend until
    smooth.

MAKES ABOUT 2 CUPS

Hummus

A fantastic-tasting Middle Eastern dish to be used as a dip
or as a filling in pita sandwiches. An excellent source of complete
protein and, now, essential fatty acids.

1 15-ounce can or 1 2/3 cups cooked garbanzo beans (chickpeas)
1/4 cup tahini (sesame seed paste)
3 tablespoons lemon juice
3 tablespoons Barlean's organic flax oil
2 medium cloves garlic
1/4 teaspoon ground coriander
1/4 teaspoon ground cumin
1/4 teaspoon paprika
dash of cayenne
1/4 cup minced scallions
2 tablespoons minced fresh parsley for garnish

- In a blender or food processor, process the garbanzo beans, tahini,
    lemon juice, and flax oil until the mixture reaches the consistency
    of a coarse paste. Use as much of the garbanzo liquid, or water, as
    needed.
- Add the garlic, coriander, cumin, paprika, and cayenne and blend
    thoroughly.
- Transfer the hummus to a bowl and stir in the scallions.
- Cover the hummus and refrigerate.
- Garnish with parsley before serving.

MAKES ABOUT 2 1/2 CUPS

Dairyless Flax Sour Cream

*An alternative for those sensitive to dairy products
or those wanting to avoid animal products. All the tang
you'd expect from sour cream.*

6 ounces silken tofu
1 tablespoon Barlean's organic flax oil
1 tablespoon nutritional yeast
2 tablespoons lemon juice
2 teaspoons rice vinegar
1 teaspoon plum vinegar
salt or salt substitute to taste
chives for garnish (optional)

- Steam the tofu for 2 minutes.
- Combine all ingredients in a blender or food processor and process on high speed for 1 minute.
- Garnish each serving with chives if desired.

MAKES 1 CUP

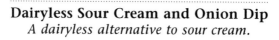

Dairyless Sour Cream and Onion Dip

A dairyless alternative to sour cream.

1/2 cup Dairyless Flax Sour Cream (page 24)
1 small clove garlic, pressed
1/2 cup minced scallions
1/2 cup Flax-Almond Mayonnaise (page 22)
1 teaspoon Worcestershire sauce

- Combine all ingredients in a blender or food processor and process until thick and creamy. Flavor is enhanced if allowed to sit awhile before serving.
- Keeps 1 to 2 days refrigerated.

MAKES 1 1/2 CUPS

Almond-Flax Butter
Produces a wonderful balance of omega-3, 6, and 9 fatty acids.
Extraordinary spread over toasted bread, as a vegetable dip,
or used in place of peanut butter.

1/2 cup raw almonds
3 tablespoons Barlean's organic flax oil

- Grind the almonds to the consistency of meal in a blender or food processor. Add the flax oil and process until creamy.

Middle Eastern Bean Dip
Rich in protein and essential fatty acids. Good as an appetizer
before a salad or vegetable meal. Use as a sandwich filling,
cracker spread, or dip for chips.

1 cup dried fava beans or whole lentils
2 tablespoons Barlean's organic flax oil
1 tablespoon lemon juice
1 clove garlic, crushed
1 tablespoon finely chopped fresh parsley
1 teaspoon raw honey
salt or salt substitute to taste
freshly ground black pepper to taste
4 pitted ripe olives for garnish

- Cover the beans generously with boiling water and leave them to soak 4 to 5 hours if possible. (Not as long if you are using lentils.) Drain and rinse.
- Place the beans or lentils in a medium saucepan with plenty of water and simmer over gentle heat until tender. (About 1 1/4 to 1 1/2 hours for beans, 30 to 45 minutes for lentils.) Drain, reserving the liquid.
- In a bowl, combine the beans or lentils with the flax oil, lemon juice, garlic, parsley, honey, salt, and pepper. Mash and mix thoroughly and, if necessary, add enough of the reserved cooking liquid to make a thick, creamy paste.
- Smooth the surface of the mixture and garnish with olives.

MAKES ABOUT 1 1/2 CUPS

Green Pea Guacamole

Can be used as an inexpensive substitute to traditional avocado guacamole. Contains healthful essential fatty acids.

1 cup green peas (fresh or frozen)
1/4 cup water (from steaming the peas)
1 jalapeño pepper, seeds removed
1/2 tablespoon lemon juice
1 tablespoon (packed) chopped fresh cilantro leaves
2 to 3 tablespoons chopped onion
2 tablespoons Barlean's organic flax oil
dash of cumin powder
dash of salt or salt substitute
2 cloves garlic, pressed
cilantro, cayenne, and a wedge of lime for garnish

- In a small pan of water, steam the peas for 3 minutes until tender. Drain, reserving 1/4 cup of the steaming water.
- Place the peas and the 1/4 cup of the steaming water in a food processor and puree. Add the remaining ingredients and puree to a thick, even consistency.
- Transfer to a small bowl and garnish with cilantro, cayenne, and a lime wedge.

SERVES 3

Eggplant Dip

Wonderful as a vegetable dip or sandwich spread.

1 eggplant
2 medium cloves garlic, crushed
1 scallion, chopped
1/4 cup chopped fresh parsley
1 tablespoon lemon juice
3 tablespoons Barlean's organic flax oil
1/2 teaspoon dried dill weed

- Bake eggplant at 400°F for 1 hour or until soft.
- Remove from oven and when cool enough to handle, peel and dice.
- Place all ingredients in a blender or food processor and process until smooth.
- Chill and serve.

MAKES ABOUT 2 CUPS

Eggplant and Tahini Cream

The subtle flavor of eggplant blends wonderfully with the rich, earthy taste of tahini. This dish is perfect with warm pita bread or crisp toast and makes a good light lunch served with soup.

2 medium eggplants (about 1 pound)
2 heaping tablespoons tahini
2 tablespoons Barlean's organic flax oil
1 tablespoon lemon juice
1 large clove garlic, crushed
salt or salt substitute to taste
freshly ground black pepper to taste
lettuce leaves
sesame seeds (optional)
fresh parsley and chives for garnish

- Prick the eggplants and bake at 400°F for 30 minutes. Let them cool, then remove the skins.
- Combine the eggplant, tahini, flax oil, lemon juice, and garlic in a blender or food processor and process until smooth.
- Season the mixture with salt and pepper to taste, then chill.
- When ready to serve, arrange a bed of lettuce leaves on a small plate and spoon the mixture on top. Sprinkle with sesame seeds and garnish with parsley and chives.

MAKES ABOUT 2¹/₂ CUPS

Spicy Pinto Bean Dip
Serve with no-oil tortilla chips.

2 1/2 cups cooked pinto beans, drained
1 1/2 tablespoons crushed garlic
2 teaspoons onion powder
3 tablespoons Barlean's organic flax oil
1 1/2 teaspoons ground cumin
2 teaspoons diced jalapeño pepper
1 teaspoon salt or salt substitute
1/4 cup water
3 tablespoons brown rice vinegar
dash of chili powder
cayenne or paprika for garnish

- Combine all ingredients in a blender or food processor and puree until smooth.
- Transfer to a bowl and garnish with cayenne or paprika.

MAKES ABOUT 3 CUPS

Thai Tomato Salsa
Serve over steamed vegetables and rice, broiled or roasted chicken, or fish.

2 scallions (3 inches of green left on), slivered lengthwise
1/3 cup lemon juice
3 tomatoes, diced
1 to 2 bunches fresh cilantro leaves, minced
3 to 4 cloves garlic, crushed
6 large basil leaves, finely chopped
1/3 large red onion, diced
1 tablespoon peeled and grated fresh ginger
1 tablespoon balsamic vinegar
1/4 cup Barlean's organic flax oil
1/4 cup extra virgin olive oil
salt or salt substitute to taste
freshly ground black pepper to taste

- Soak the scallions in the lemon juice for 30 minutes. Drain, reserving half of the lemon juice.
- Mince the scallions.
- In a medium bowl, combine the scallions, reserved lemon juice, and the remaining ingredients.

MAKES ABOUT 2 CUPS

Spinach-Mushroom Dip

*Can be served as an appetizer on crackers, as a filling
for sandwiches, or as a dip for chips.*

1 clove garlic, crushed
1 cup chopped onion
1/2 pound mushrooms, cleaned and chopped
1 tablespoon butter
1 1/4 cups spinach (or 10 ounces frozen)
1/4 cup broth or white wine
1 cup water
1/2 cup tahini
1 teaspoon salt or salt substitute
1/4 cup nutritional yeast flakes
4 tablespoons Barlean's organic flax oil
3 tablespoons lemon juice
1/8 teaspoon cayenne
1/2 teaspoon dried dill weed

- Sauté the garlic, onion, and mushrooms in the butter over low heat until soft.
- Steam the spinach until wilted.
- Combine all ingredients in a blender or food processor and puree until creamy.
- Chill and serve.

MAKES ABOUT 4 CUPS

Sunflower Seed Dressing

1 cup hulled sunflower seeds
1/2 cup Barlean's organic flax oil
1/4 cup lemon juice
1/2 cup soft tofu
1 tablespoon soy sauce or tamari
1/2 tablespoon water
1/2 teaspoon dried basil
1/2 teaspoon dried thyme

- Combine all ingredients in a blender or food processor and process until creamy.

MAKES ABOUT 2 CUPS

Basil Dressing

1/4 cup Barlean's organic flax oil
1/4 cup water
3 tablespoons lemon juice
2 tablespoons fresh basil or 2 teaspoons dried basil
1 teaspoon finely chopped garlic
freshly ground black pepper to taste

- Combine all ingredients in a blender or food processor and blend thoroughly.

MAKES ABOUT 3/4 CUP

Lemon-Tarragon Dressing

1/4 cup lemon juice
2 tablespoons water
1 teaspoon Dijon mustard
cayenne to taste
2 tablespoons Barlean's organic flax oil
1 1/2 teaspoons chopped fresh tarragon or 1/2 teaspoon dried tarragon

- Combine the lemon juice, water, mustard, and cayenne in a blender and blend thoroughly. Add the flax oil and tarragon and blend well.

MAKES 1/2 CUP

Green Goddess Taiwanese Style

Try over salads or as a dip for Thai spring rolls.

1 1/2 tablespoons peanut butter
1 tablespoon golden miso
1 teaspoon peeled and chopped fresh ginger
3/4 cup water
1 tablespoon rice vinegar
2 tablespoons Barlean's organic flax oil
1/4 teaspoon red chili flakes
1/2 cup chopped scallions
1 teaspoon raw honey
3 tablespoons lime juice

- Combine all ingredients in a blender or food processor and process until creamy.

MAKES ABOUT 1 3/4 CUPS

Oregano Dressing

3 tablespoons red wine vinegar or rice vinegar
1 tablespoon water
1 tablespoon lemon juice
3 tablespoons Barlean's organic flax oil
2 tablespoons minced fresh parsley
1 tablespoon chopped fresh oregano or 3/4 teaspoon dried oregano
freshly ground black pepper to taste

- Combine all ingredients in a blender and blend thoroughly.

MAKES 3/4 CUP

Miso-Ginger Dressing

1 cup water
1 1/2 tablespoons mellow white miso
1 tablespoon tahini
2 cloves garlic, chopped
1/2 tablespoon peeled and chopped fresh ginger
1 tablespoon lemon juice
1/2 scallion, chopped
3 tablespoons Barlean's organic flax oil

- Combine all ingredients in a blender or food processor and process until creamy.

MAKES 1 1/3 CUPS

Cucumber-Dill Dressing

2 tablespoons lemon juice
3 tablespoons Barlean's organic flax oil
2 tablespoons extra virgin olive oil
1 medium cucumber, peeled and diced
1 tablespoon mayonnaise or eggless mayonnaise
1/4 teaspoon dry mustard
2 teaspoons dried dill weed or 2 tablespoons fresh dill
1/4 teaspoon salt or salt substitute

- Combine all ingredients in a blender or food processor and process to a creamy consistency.

MAKES ABOUT 1 CUP

Herbal Bouquet Salad Dressing

2 cloves garlic, crushed
$1/4$ cup Barlean's organic flax oil
$1/4$ cup extra virgin olive oil
4 tablespoons lemon juice
$1/2$ teaspoon dried basil
$1/2$ teaspoon dried chervil
$1/4$ teaspoon dried thyme
$1/4$ teaspoon dried oregano
$1/2$ teaspoon dried savory
$1/4$ teaspoon ground coriander
$1/8$ teaspoon dried sage
salt or salt substitute to taste
2 teaspoons Dijon mustard
1 tablespoon mayonnaise or eggless mayonnaise

- Combine all ingredients in a blender or food processor and process to an even consistency.

MAKES ABOUT $3/4$ CUP

Creamy Garlic Dressing
A dairyless salad dressing that mimics the richness and texture of sour cream.

$1/4$ cup water
1 medium clove garlic, crushed
4 ounces soft tofu or silken tofu
$1/4$ cup Barlean's organic flax oil
3 tablespoons lemon juice
2 teaspoons rice vinegar
1 teaspoon kelp
1 tablespoon poppy seeds
1 teaspoon dried dill weed
seasoned salt or salt substitute to taste (optional)

- Combine all ingredients in a blender or food processor and process to an even consistency.

MAKES $1 1/2$ CUPS

Lemon–Poppy Seed Dressing

1 1/2 tablespoons poppy seeds
2 1/2 tablespoons lemon juice
1 teaspoon raw honey
2 tablespoons mayonnaise or eggless mayonnaise
1/2 teaspoon dry mustard
1 1/2 tablespoons Barlean's organic flax oil

- Combine all ingredients and whisk vigorously.

MAKES ABOUT 3/4 CUP

Tomato Salad Dressing

1/2 cup tomato juice
1/4 cup Barlean's organic flax oil
1/4 cup extra virgin olive oil
3 tablespoons lemon juice
1/2 teaspoon dried basil
1/4 teaspoon dried oregano
1 clove garlic, crushed

- Combine all ingredients in a blender or food processor and blend for 2 minutes.

MAKES ABOUT 1 CUP

Cilantro Dressing
Flavorful with accents of the southwest.

3 tablespoons tahini
1 1/2 tablespoons miso
1 large clove garlic
3/4 cup water
1/4 cup rice vinegar
1/3 cup (packed) fresh cilantro leaves
dash of hot chili sauce
2 tablespoons Barlean's organic flax oil

- Combine all ingredients in a blender or food processor and process until creamy.

MAKES 1 1/3 CUPS

Dreamy Creamy Avocado Dressing

1 large ripe avocado, diced
1 medium cucumber, peeled and cut in chunks
2 teaspoons dried dill weed
seasoned salt or salt-free seasoning to taste
1 tablespoon lime juice
2 tablespoons Barlean's organic flax oil

- Combine all ingredients in a blender or food processor and process to a smooth, even consistency.

MAKES ABOUT 1 1/2 CUPS

Herb Oil

Serve on fish, potatoes, and vegetables. Expensive Italian restaurants serve warm herbed oil to dip bread into. Try it, it's a real treat!

1/2 teaspoon dried savory
1/2 teaspoon dried marjoram
1/2 teaspoon dried basil
1/2 teaspoon dried tarragon
1 tablespoon minced fresh parsley
1 tablespoon minced chives
1 clove garlic, crushed
1/4 teaspoon paprika
1/4 cup Barlean's organic flax oil

- Pulverize the dried herbs by rubbing between palms of hands.
- Combine all ingredients. Store in a covered jar and keep in the refrigerator.

MAKES ABOUT 1/4 CUP
Contributed by Dr. Jack Tips, N.D., *The Pro Vita Plan*

Orange–Sesame Seed Dressing

3/4 cup orange juice (about 2 oranges juiced)
1/4 cup Barlean's organic flax oil
3 tablespoons sesame seeds

- Combine all ingredients in a mixing bowl and whisk vigorously, or place ingredients in a blender or food processor and blend thoroughly.

MAKES ABOUT 1 CUP

Rich and Creamy Cheesy Dressing
A cheesy dressing without the cheese. An excellent choice
for those wishing to avoid dairy products but looking for the taste
and consistency of cheese.

3 tablespoons Barlean's organic flax oil
3 tablespoons extra virgin olive oil
3 tablespoons lemon juice
1 large clove garlic, crushed
2 teaspoons sesame or poppy seeds
2 tablespoons tahini
2 tablespoons eggless mayonnaise
5 tablespoons water
dash of Worcestershire sauce (optional)
dash of cayenne
dash of salt (optional)
freshly ground black pepper

- Measure ingredients into a salad bowl. Whisk until thick and creamy.

SERVES 4 TO 6 (MAKES ABOUT 1 CUP)

Creamy Dijon Dressing

4 ounces firm tofu
1/4 cup Barlean's organic flax oil
1 medium clove garlic, crushed
1 small tomato
2 teaspoons soy sauce or tamari
3 tablespoons water
1/2 teaspoon Dijon mustard
2 1/4 tablespoons rice vinegar
3 tablespoons lemon juice
1 tablespoon apple cider vinegar
1 1-inch chunk onion
1 tablespoon minced chives
2 teaspoons dried dill weed
1/4 teaspoon salt or salt substitute

- Combine all ingredients in a blender or food processor and process
  to a creamy consistency.

MAKES 1 1/2 CUPS

Tahini Dressing

1 tablespoon Barlean's organic flax oil
1 1/2 tablespoons tahini
3 tablespoons water
1 tablespoon lime juice
1 1-inch chunk red onion
1 tablespoon tamari

- Combine all ingredients in a blender or food processor and process to an even consistency.

MAKES 1/2 CUP

Tahini-Mint Dressing

2 tablespoons tahini
2 cloves garlic, pressed
1 tablespoon dried mint or 2 tablespoons fresh mint
1/2 cup water
1 tablespoon lemon juice
1 teaspoon white miso
2 tablespoons Barlean's organic flax oil

- Combine all ingredients in a blender or food processor and process until smooth.

MAKES 3/4 CUP

Curried Salad Dressing
Prepared directly in a salad bowl, just add mixed greens and vegetables of your choice.

2 tablespoons Barlean's organic flax oil
1 tablespoon lemon juice
1 to 2 tablespoons eggless mayonnaise
1 teaspoon raw honey
1/2 teaspoon curry powder
1/2 teaspoon dried basil or 2 teaspoons fresh basil
1 teaspoon minced scallions
1/4 teaspoon salt or 1/2 teaspoon kelp powder
freshly ground black pepper

- Measure ingredients into a salad bowl. Whisk until thick and creamy.

SERVES 2 (MAKES ABOUT 1/4 CUP)

4

Salads

ADD VIM AND VIGOR TO YOUR SALADS
WITH FATTY ACID–RICH OIL

FLAX FOR THOUGHT Salads are generally referred to as healthy. Commercially prepared salads may contain ingredients that include the bad "funny fats" (hydrogenated oils). In addition, commercially available salad dressings almost always use highly refined oils as their primary ingredient. The result is that salads are not nearly as healthful as they could be. By preparing salads at home and using flax oil as an ingredient in place of less healthful oils, you can significantly boost the levels of essential fatty acids in your diet while restricting less healthful fats and oils.

Another benefit of adding flax oil to your favorite salad recipes is that the essential fatty acids cause a feeling of fullness and lasting satisfaction following their ingestion. This phenomenon may limit the calories consumed at a sitting—aiding in diet, weight loss, or maintenance programs. In this way, a salad prepared with flax oil and eaten with one of the soups in Chapter 5 could be experienced as a complete, healthful, and satisfying meal.

Brown Rice and Spinach Salad
Hearty and healthy.

2 teaspoons extra virgin olive oil
1 tablespoon minced scallions
4 cups chopped fresh spinach
2 tablespoons Barlean's organic flax oil
2 teaspoons lemon juice
2 teaspoons rice vinegar
2 tablespoons soy sauce or tamari
4 cups cooked brown rice

- Heat the olive oil in a skillet. Add the scallions and sauté until soft, adding a few teaspoons of water to prevent browning. Add the spinach and braise until soft. Set aside.
- In large bowl, combine the flax oil, lemon juice, rice vinegar, and soy sauce. Stir in the rice and the spinach mixture.

SERVES 4

Marinated Cauliflower Salad
A perfect harmony of cruciferous vegetables.

Salad
1 large head cauliflower, cored and sliced
1 cup sliced green olives
1 green bell pepper, cut into thin strips
1 medium onion, chopped
1/4 cup or 2 ounces finely chopped pimentos

Marinade
1/4 cup Barlean's organic flax oil
juice of 1/2 lemon
3 tablespoons white wine vinegar
2 teaspoons salt or salt substitute
1/2 teaspoon raw honey
1/4 teaspoon black pepper

- Combine the salad ingredients in a large bowl.
- Mix together the marinade ingredients and pour over the salad. Refrigerate overnight.

SERVES 4

Fruit Salad with Flax-Maple Dressing

1 fresh pineapple, cut into 1-inch pieces
2 golden delicious apples, pared, cored, and sliced
1 ripe pear, pared, cored, and sliced
1 banana, sliced
1 cup sliced strawberries
2 tablespoons Barlean's organic flax oil
2 tablespoons pure maple syrup
1/4 cup apple juice
1/4 cup chopped pitted dates (optional)
1/4 cup golden raisins (optional)
romaine lettuce leaves
plain nonfat yogurt to top (optional)

- Combine the pineapple, apples, pear, banana, and strawberries in a bowl.
- In another bowl, combine the flax oil, maple syrup, and apple juice and whisk to an even consistency. Add the dates and raisins.
- Combine the two mixtures. Toss lightly to moisten all of the fruit pieces. Cover and refrigerate for 30 minutes.
- When ready to serve, line a salad bowl with the lettuce leaves and arrange the salad on top.
- If desired, top with yogurt.

SERVES 4

Tuna Salad Supreme

Packed with protein and rich in essential fatty acids.

1 6 1/4-ounce can water-packed, no-salt tuna, drained
1 scallion, chopped
2 red radishes, sliced
1 stalk celery, chopped
1 tablespoon no-salt mustard
1 tablespoon Barlean's organic flax oil
1/8 teaspoon cayenne

- Place tuna in a medium bowl and cover with onion, radishes, celery, mustard, flax oil, and cayenne. Mix together well.
- Serve with a sprig of parsley or use as a sandwich spread.

SERVES 1 TO 2

This recipe comes compliments of *The Fat Burning Diet,* authored by fitness expert Mr. Jay Robb.

Mediterranean Salad

1 cucumber, sliced
1 bunch radishes, trimmed
1 red bell pepper, cut into strips
1 green bell pepper, cut into wedges
3 tomatoes, cut into wedges
1/2 bunch chicory or curly endive lettuce, shredded
6 scallions, sliced
3 tablespoons Oregano Dressing (page 31)
2 tablespoons crumbled feta cheese

- In a medium bowl, combine the cucumber, radishes, bell peppers, tomatoes, chicory or lettuce, and scallions. Add the Oregano Dressing and toss to coat well.
- Sprinkle with feta cheese.

SERVES 4

Hearty Vegetable Salad

1 tablespoon Barlean's organic flax oil
1/2 cup red wine vinegar
1/3 cup chopped fresh parsley
2 tablespoons lemon juice
1 clove garlic, minced
2 teaspoons dried basil, crumbled
3/4 teaspoon salt or salt substitute
1/4 teaspoon freshly ground pepper
3 large boiling potatoes, peeled, cooked, and thinly sliced
1 1/2 pounds baby carrots, cooked
1 1/2 pounds green beans, cooked and cut to same length as carrots
3 beets, cooked and thinly sliced
lettuce leaves

- Mix together the flax oil, vinegar, parsley, lemon juice, garlic, basil, salt, and pepper.
- Place the potatoes, carrots, and beans in one bowl and the beets in a smaller bowl. Pour the vinaigrette over the vegetables and stir gently.
- Cover and let marinate for 3 hours at room temperature or refrigerate overnight.
- When ready to serve, line a platter with the lettuce leaves and arrange the vegetables on top.

SERVES 6

Avocado, Jicama, and Grapefruit Salad
A colorful array of fruit and vegetables that are
pleasing to the eye and palate.

1 large or 2 small avocados
2 medium ruby red grapefruit
1/2 pound jicama
2 tablespoons Barlean's organic flax oil
1 tablespoon minced fresh parsley

- Peel the avocados and cut into wedges. Peel the grapefruit and cut into sections, reserving the juice. Peel the jicama and cut into thin wedges the same length as the avocado slices.
- On 4 individual plates, alternate slices of avocado, grapefruit, and jicama and arrange in a circle or fan.
- Combine the flax oil, reserved grapefruit juice, and parsley in a small bowl. Drizzle over the salads.

SERVES 4

Lentil Salad

1 cup dried lentils
2 quarts water
1 bay leaf
1 clove garlic, minced
1 teaspoon salt or salt substitute
1/4 cup scallions
1/2 cup chopped fresh parsley
1 teaspoon prepared mustard
1/2 teaspoon black pepper
1 tablespoon Barlean's organic flax oil
1 tablespoon lemon juice
1/2 cup grated carrot for garnish

- Clean the lentils and place in a large pot with the water, bay leaf, garlic, and salt. Heat to boiling. Turn the heat off and let sit for 30 minutes. Drain and remove the bay leaf.
- Transfer to a bowl. Add the scallions, parsley, mustard, pepper, flax oil, and lemon juice and mix thoroughly.
- Garnish with grated carrot.

SERVES 4

Rice, Bean, and Corn Salad

This extremely nutritious and hearty salad can be used
as an entrée, especially during the hot summer months.

2 cups cooked brown rice
1 16-ounce can or 2 cups cooked red kidney beans, drained and rinsed
1^1/$_2$ cups cooked fresh corn or thawed frozen corn
4 scallions, chopped
^{1}/$_8$ cup Barlean's organic flax oil
^{1}/$_8$ cup lime juice
^{1}/$_8$ cup cider vinegar
1 tablespoon brown sugar
2 fresh or pickled jalapeño peppers, minced
1 teaspoon chili powder
^{1}/$_2$ teaspoon ground cumin
^{1}/$_2$ teaspoon salt or salt substitute
wedges of lime

- Mix together and serve with lime wedges.

SERVES 4

Divine Carrot-Currant Salad

As a side dish or main meal, this sweet carrot salad is sure to please.

^{1}/$_2$ cup currants
^{1}/$_2$ cup boiling water
2 tablespoons tahini
2 tablespoons Barlean's organic flax oil
1 tablespoon lemon juice
2 teaspoons raw honey
dash of cinnamon
^{1}/$_2$ cup grated carrot

- Soak the currants in the boiling water for 1 or more hours. Drain and reserve the currant water.
- Combine the currant water, tahini, flax oil, lemon juice, honey, and cinnamon in a food processor or blender and process until creamy.
- Place the carrot and currants in a bowl. Pour the dressing over the salad and mix well.

SERVES 2

Zucchini and Caper Salad

This is a great summer salad for using the abundance
of fresh zucchini produced in a home garden.

4 large zucchini, quartered lengthwise, then cut into 1/2-inch slices
1 small red bell pepper, seeded and finely chopped
2 tablespoons capers, rinsed
1 tablespoon chopped fresh parsley
1 tablespoon Barlean's organic flax oil
1 tablespoon lemon juice
1/2 teaspoon dry mustard
1/4 teaspoon black pepper
1 head red leaf lettuce, leaves separated

- In a medium bowl, combine the zucchini, bell pepper, capers, and parsley.
- In a small bowl, combine the flax oil, lemon juice, mustard, and pepper and blend thoroughly.
- Pour the dressing over the zucchini mixture and toss to coat well.
- Line 4 individual serving bowls with the lettuce. Place the zucchini mixture in the centers just before the salads are to be served.

SERVES 4

Caesar Salad

1/2 clove garlic, crushed
3 tablespoons Barlean's organic flax oil
1/2 teaspoon dry mustard
1 tablespoon lemon juice
1 tablespoon white wine vinegar
2 teaspoons soy sauce or tamari
6 Greek olives, pitted and chopped into a paste
2 bunches romaine lettuce, washed, dried, and torn into bite-size pieces
1 cup whole-grain croutons

- In a jar with a tight fitting lid, combine the garlic, flax oil, mustard, lemon juice, vinegar, soy sauce, and olive paste. Secure the lid and shake until the dressing is emulsified.
- Place the lettuce in a large salad bowl and toss with the dressing. Sprinkle with croutons and serve immediately.

SERVES 4

Vegetable Rice Salad

*This delicious and spicy salad works very well
with Indian and East Asian dishes.*

Salad

2 cups cooked long-grain brown rice

1/4 cup finely sliced radish (about 3 large radishes)

1/2 cup peeled, seeded, and finely diced cucumber

1/2 cup finely diced red bell pepper

1/4 cup finely diced celery

1/4 cup thinly sliced scallions

Dressing

2 tablespoons extra virgin olive oil

2 tablespoons Barlean's organic flax oil

1/4 cup freshly grated Parmesan cheese

3 tablespoons cider vinegar

2 tablespoons plain nonfat yogurt

1 tablespoon minced fresh basil, or other fresh herb

1/2 teaspoon prepared mustard

Garnish

lettuce leaves

tomato wedges

2 tablespoons pumpkin seeds (optional)

- Combine all of the salad ingredients in a large bowl.
- Blend all of the dressing ingredients in a small mixing bowl.
- Add the dressing to the salad and mix well. Cover tightly and refrigerate overnight.
- When ready to serve, arrange the lettuce leaves on a large serving platter. Toss the salad lightly and mound it in the center. Garnish with tomato wedges. Sprinkle with pumpkin seeds if desired.

SERVES 6

Taco Salad

Dressing

1/4 green bell pepper, very finely chopped
1 scallion, finely chopped
2 tablespoons finely chopped cilantro
3 tablespoons Barlean's organic flax oil
1 tablespoon white vinegar
1 tablespoon lemon juice
1/4 teaspoon salt
1/4 teaspoon chili powder
1/2 clove garlic, crushed

Salad

1 head green leaf lettuce, washed and broken into bite-size pieces
1/4 cup sliced black olives
1 tomato, diced
1/2 cup broken tortilla chips or corn chips

Toppings

guacamole
6 whole black olives

- Combine the dressing ingredients in a small bowl. Whisk and allow to sit for 30 minutes.
- In a large salad bowl, mix the salad ingredients. Cover with the dressing and toss.
- Serve in large individual salad dishes. Place a generous dab of guacamole on top and garnish with a whole black olive.

SERVES 6

Tabouli
A zesty and healthful Middle Eastern grain dish.

1 cup bulgur wheat
2 cups boiling water
2 tomatoes, finely diced
1 bunch scallions with tops, finely chopped
1 cup finely chopped fresh parsley
3 tablespoons chopped fresh mint leaves or 2 teaspoons dried mint
1/4 cup lemon juice
2 tablespoons Barlean's organic flax oil
1/4 teaspoon black pepper
1/4 teaspoon dried oregano
1/4 teaspoon ground cumin
1/4 teaspoon allspice
1/4 teaspoon coriander

- Place the bulgur in a medium bowl and pour the boiling water over the bulgur. Let soak for 1 hour.
- Drain well, pressing out the excess water through a fine strainer or cheesecloth.
- Add the tomatoes, scallions, parsley, and mint to the bulgur and mix thoroughly. Set aside.
- In a small bowl, combine the lemon juice, flax oil, pepper, oregano, cumin, allspice, and coriander.
- Pour the dressing over the bulgur mixture and toss to coat well. Marinate for 1 hour before serving.

SERVES 6

Corn Salad

2 24-ounce bags frozen corn
8 ounces Monterey jack or soy cheese, diced
1 large red bell pepper, diced
1 large green bell pepper, diced
1 red onion, diced
3 tablespoons Barlean's organic flax oil
3 tablespoons white wine vinegar
1 tablespoon ground cumin
1 teaspoon salt or salt substitute
1/2 teaspoon black pepper
1/8 teaspoon cayenne

- Cook corn according to package directions. Drain and rinse with cold water.
- Place in a large bowl. Add the cheese, bell peppers, and onion. Toss well.
- Combine the flax oil, vinegar, cumin, salt, pepper, and cayenne in a jar with a tight fitting lid. Shake well.
- Pour the dressing over the corn mixture and mix well. Cover and refrigerate at least 3 hours (or overnight), stirring occasionally.

SERVES 6

Waldorf Salad

*This is a fantastic salad, from both taste
and nutritional perspectives.*

Dressing

10 ounces firm tofu

1/2 cup plain nonfat yogurt

3 tablespoons raw honey

2 tablespoons Barlean's organic flax oil

2 tablespoons lemon juice

juice of 1 orange

1/2 teaspoon ground cloves, cinnamon, nutmeg, or cardamom

1/4 teaspoon vanilla extract (optional)

Salad

2 apples, chopped

2 pears, chopped

4 stalks celery, chopped

1/2 cup raisins

- In a blender or food processor, process all of the dressing ingredients until smooth and creamy. The dressing may be refrigerated for up to a week. (Makes about 2 cups of dressing.)

- Mix the salad ingredients together and toss with the dressing. Serve chilled.

SERVES 4

5

Sauces and Soups

BOOSTING THE NUTRITIONAL VALUE
OF SAUCES AND SOUPS THE FLAX WAY

FLAX FOR THOUGHT Most of the sauces and soups you find on grocery store shelves contain some form of fat for flavor and texture. Unfortunately, the fats and oils they contain are either highly saturated or health-robbing hydrogenated oils. On the other hand, the no-fat and low-fat brands are completely devoid of the essential good fats and lack the flavor and texture that fats and oils bring to sauces and soups. The solution to obtaining truly healthful sauces and soups is to make them from scratch with flax oil, which will impart greater taste satisfaction and satiety.

Here are some simple improvisations for adding flax oil to sauces and soups.

- Replace less healthful oils in your favorite sauce and soup recipes with an equal amount of flax oil, stirring it in after the sauce or soup has been heated or cooked. If the taste of flax oil is too strong for you, use 1/2 extra virgin olive oil and 1/2 flax oil. (I recommend extra virgin olive oil because it is not subjected to the damaging manufacturing practices common to other grocery store oils.)

- If you are not a cook, you can easily incorporate flax oil into premade sauces and soups by simply stirring some in after the sauce or soup has been heated or cooked. It's a good way to get your flax on the run.

Sesame Sauce
An uncooked sauce perfect over pasta or grains.

1/2 cup sesame seeds
1 teaspoon minced garlic
1/2 teaspoon peeled and crushed fresh ginger (crush through a garlic press)
3 tablespoons Barlean's organic flax oil
3 tablespoons extra virgin olive oil
1 teaspoon sesame oil
1/8 teaspoon red pepper flakes
6 tablespoons soy sauce or tamari
1 tablespoon powdered vegetable broth
1/2 cup water

- Lightly toast the sesame seeds for 1 minute in a frying pan.
- In a blender or food processor, combine the ingredients in descending order, processing after every 3 additions. Process the entire mixture until thick.

MAKES 1 3/4 CUPS

Sweet and Sour Sauce
Excellent when coupled with brown rice and mixed vegetables.

2 tablespoons Barlean's organic flax oil
2 tablespoons ketchup or tomato sauce
1/4 cup water
1 tablespoon soy sauce or tamari
1 tablespoon vinegar
2 teaspoons raw honey
2 teaspoons arrowroot

- Combine all ingredients and whisk or blend thoroughly.

MAKES ABOUT 1/2 CUP

Mushroom Stroganoff
Excellent over pasta. Try over whole grains, too!

1 tablespoon extra virgin olive oil
1 medium onion, chopped (about 1¹/2 cups)
1 medium clove garlic, crushed
¹/2 pound mushrooms, thinly sliced (about 4 cups)
3 tablespoons lemon juice
¹/2 teaspoon dried tarragon
¹/2 teaspoon paprika
freshly ground black pepper
³/4 cup vegetable broth or water
1 tablespoon tahini
2 tablespoons Barlean's organic flax oil
1 small tomato, peeled, seeded, and diced (optional)

- Heat the olive oil in a skillet. Add the onion and garlic and sauté until soft. Add the mushrooms and sauté until the mushrooms soften. Add the lemon juice, tarragon, paprika, and pepper. Mix well.
- Blend the vegetable broth and tahini. Pour over the mushroom mixture and mix well.
- Remove from heat. Add the flax oil and tomato and stir until an even consistency is achieved.

SERVES 2

Flax Gravy
Great over mashed potatoes. A creamy gravy with no compromise.

3 cups potato water or water
2 tablespoons powdered vegetable broth or 2 vegetable bouillon cubes
3 cups whole wheat flour
3 tablespoons Barlean's organic flax oil

- Heat the water in a pot, whisking in the vegetable broth or bouillon cubes until dissolved.
- Slowly whisk in the flour, over medium-high heat, stirring until gravy thickens to desired consistency.
- Remove from heat and cool to serving temperature.
- Stir in the flax oil and serve.

MAKES 3 CUPS

Onion Sauce

A wonderful compliment to freshly steamed veggies, a perfect
butter-free dip for artichokes, and a winner with broccoli.

2 tablespoons extra virgin olive oil
1 medium white onion, thinly sliced (1 cup packed)
1/4 teaspoon ground thyme
1 cup water
4 teaspoons powdered vegetable broth or miso, or 1 vegetable
  bouillon cube
2 tablespoons Barlean's organic flax oil

- Heat the olive oil in a skillet. Add the onion and thyme. Sauté, stir-ring for 3 to 4 minutes, until the onion begins to brown. Add the water and powdered vegetable broth, miso, or bouillon cube. Bring to a boil and simmer 3 to 4 minutes over high heat.
- Puree in a blender or food processor. Add the flax oil and blend briefly to combine.

MAKES 1 1/2 CUPS

Onion Gravy with Tarragon

1 tablespoon extra virgin olive oil
1 large onion, sliced
1 1/2 cups water
2 teaspoons powdered vegetable broth or 1 vegetable bouillon cube
1/4 teaspoon dried tarragon
1/4 teaspoon dried sage
1/4 teaspoon dried chervil
dash of nutmeg
2 tablespoons Barlean's organic flax oil

- Heat the olive oil in a medium pan over high heat. Add the onion and sauté, stirring frequently, until the onion is browned. Stir in the water and powdered broth or bouillon cube. Add the tarragon, sage, chervil, and nutmeg. Bring to a boil, lower heat to medium, and simmer gravy until liquid is reduced.
- Remove from heat and cool to serving temperature.
- Stir in the flax oil and serve.

MAKES ABOUT 2 CUPS

Creamy Mushroom-Onion Gravy
Can't be beat over mashed potatoes or your favorite whole grains.

1 tablespoon extra virgin olive oil
1 white onion, diced
1 small clove garlic, crushed
1 cup sliced mushrooms
1 tablespoon whole wheat flour
3 tablespoons nutritional yeast (optional)
1$^1/_2$ cups potato water or water
1$^1/_2$ tablespoons powdered vegetable broth or 2 vegetable bouillon
  cubes
2$^1/_2$ tablespoons Barlean's organic flax oil

- Heat the olive oil in a medium pot. Add the onion and garlic and sauté until soft, about 3 to 4 minutes. Add the mushrooms and sauté 2 to 3 minutes longer, stirring occasionally. Stir in the flour and yeast. Slowly add the water, stirring with a whisk to dissolve lumps until smooth. Add the vegetable broth or crumbled bouillon cubes and continue to stir. Allow gravy to simmer and thicken over medium heat for 5 minutes.
- Remove from heat and cool to serving temperature.
- Stir in the flax oil and serve.

MAKES 2$^1/_2$ CUPS

Southwestern Sauce
*Inspired by the flavors of New Mexico. Try as a
chip dip, taco sauce, or over enchiladas.*

2 tablespoons lemon juice
$^1/_2$ cup green chilies, braised in oven
$^1/_4$ cup rice vinegar
$^1/_2$ cup water
3 tablespoons nutritional yeast
$^1/_4$ teaspoon salt or salt substitute
$^1/_2$ teaspoon ground cumin
2 tablespoons Barlean's organic flax oil
1 teaspoon raw honey

- Combine all ingredients in a blender or food processor and process to an even consistency.

MAKES 1$^1/_4$ CUPS

Spicy Cauliflower Sauce
A perfect compliment to Mexican dishes,
especially delicious over enchiladas.

1 medium cauliflower, chopped
1/2 cup (packed) fresh cilantro leaves
2 cloves garlic
2 tablespoons Barlean's organic flax oil
1 jalapeño pepper
1 teaspoon soy sauce or tamari
1 cup water

- Steam the cauliflower until tender, about 15 minutes.
- Place the cauliflower in a blender or food processor with the remaining ingredients. Puree until creamy.
- Serve hot.

MAKES 2 CUPS

Szechwan Peanut Sauce
Delicious over pasta and grains, or use as a dip
for vegetables or spring rolls.

1 medium clove garlic, crushed
1 teaspoon minced fresh ginger or 1/2 teaspoon dried ginger
1 tablespoon minced scallions
6 tablespoons peanut butter
2 tablespoons soy sauce or tamari
2 tablespoons raw honey
1 teaspoon dry mustard
1 tablespoon barbecue sauce
2 tablespoons Barlean's organic flax oil
1/3 cup vegetable stock or water

- Combine all ingredients in a food processor or blender and process to desired consistency.

MAKES ABOUT 1 CUP

Pumpkin Seed–Mint Sauce
Delicious over your favorite grains or vegetables.

2 tablespoons mayonnaise or eggless mayonnaise
1 cup hot water
1/4 cup pumpkin seeds, toasted lightly
2 large green serrano chilies, seeded and chopped
1/2 teaspoon onion powder
1/2 teaspoon salt or salt substitute
2 tablespoons dried mint or 3 tablespoons fresh mint
3 cloves garlic, crushed
3 tablespoons Barlean's organic flax oil
freshly ground black pepper to taste

- Combine all ingredients in a blender or food processor and process until creamy.

MAKES ABOUT 1 1/2 CUPS

No-Cream of Broccoli Soup

1 medium onion, sliced
1 medium carrot, sliced
1 stalk celery, sliced
1 clove garlic
1 cup vegetable broth or water
2 cups chopped broccoli
1/2 cup macaroni
1 cup soy milk, rice milk, or nonfat milk
1/8 teaspoon cayenne
1/8 teaspoon peeled and grated fresh ginger
1/2 teaspoon salt or salt substitute
2 tablespoons Barlean's organic flax oil

- In a covered pot, simmer the onion, carrot, celery, garlic, and vegetable broth for 5 minutes.
- Add the broccoli and macaroni and simmer another 5 to 10 minutes.
- Transfer to a blender. Add the milk, cayenne, ginger, salt, and flax oil and puree.

SERVES 4

Gazpacho

A chilled soup referred to by many as the "Spanish salad soup."

1 large onion, chopped
2 large cloves garlic, crushed
1 28-ounce can tomatoes
3 tablespoons Barlean's organic flax oil
2 teaspoons wine vinegar
1¹/2 teaspoons salt or substitute
freshly ground black pepper
1 cucumber
1 small green or red bell pepper
1 tablespoon chopped fresh chives
1 tablespoon chopped fresh mint
croutons to top

- Place the onion, garlic, tomatoes, flax oil, vinegar, salt, and a grinding of pepper in a blender or food processor and puree.
- Refrigerate about 2 hours.
- Just before serving the soup, peel the cucumber and remove the seeds from the bell pepper. Chop both into small pieces and stir into the soup, along with the freshly chopped herbs.
- Ladle into individual bowls. Top with croutons.

SERVES 4

Tomato Soup

3 cups finely chopped fresh tomatoes
1 medium onion, finely chopped
2 stalks celery, finely chopped
1 large carrot, grated
1 quart vegetable stock or water
³/4 teaspoon dried oregano
1¹/2 teaspoons dried basil
2 tablespoons Barlean's organic flax oil
freshly ground black pepper to taste

- Place the tomatoes, onion, celery, carrot, and vegetable stock in a soup pot. Bring to a boil, then reduce the heat to medium-low. Add the oregano and basil and simmer until the vegetables are tender.
- Remove from heat and stir in the flax oil. Season with pepper.

SERVES 4

Barley Vegetable Soup

A hearty soup, especially warming after outdoor activity on a brisk fall day.

1/4 cup washed whole barley
6 cups boiling water
1 cup sliced carrots
1/2 cup diced celery
1/4 cup chopped onion
2 cups skinned and chopped tomatoes
1 cup peas (fresh or frozen)
3 tablespoons Barlean's organic flax oil
1/2 cup chopped fresh parsley
salt or salt substitute to taste

- Place the barley and water in a heavy kettle. Cover and simmer until the barley is tender, about 1 hour.
- Add the remaining ingredients, except the flax oil and parsley. Cover and cook until the vegetables are barely tender.
- Remove from heat and stir in the flax oil and parsley. Season to taste.

SERVES 6

Spinach and Parsnip Soup

2 cups water
3 medium parsnips, chopped
1 small onion, chopped
1 bunch fresh spinach, finely chopped, or 10-ounce package frozen
    chopped spinach
1 cup chopped mushrooms
1 tablespoon curry powder
1 teaspoon dried chervil
1/2 teaspoon cinnamon
1/4 cup chopped fresh parsley
2 tablespoons Barlean's organic flax oil

- In a soup pot, cook the parsnips and onion in the water until very tender.
- Mash or puree in a blender.
- Return to heat. If the mixture is too thick, add more water.
- In a saucepan, cook the spinach and mushrooms until very tender.
- Mash or puree in a blender, then pour into the parsnip mixture.
- Add the herbs and spices. Stir in the flax oil and serve.

SERVES 4

Carrot and Parsnip Soup with Vegetables

6 medium carrots, chopped
1 large parsnip, chopped
1 small onion, chopped
2 cloves garlic, minced
3 cups water
1 cup chopped broccoli
1 cup chopped asparagus
1 cup chopped zucchini
1 cup peas (fresh or frozen)
1 sprig fresh parsley, finely chopped
1 teaspoon ground cumin
1 teaspoon dried sweet marjoram
1 teaspoon dried basil
1/2 teaspoon white pepper
4 tablespoons Barlean's organic flax oil

- In a soup pot, cook the carrots, parsnip, onion, and garlic in the water until very tender.
- Mash, or transfer to a blender or food processor and puree.
- Return to medium heat, adding water if the mixture is too thick. Add the remaining ingredients, except the flax oil, and cook until tender, but not mushy.
- Remove from heat and stir in the flax oil.

SERVES 6

Sweet Potato–Pumpkin Soup

1/2 quart peeled sweet potatoes, cut into chunks

1/2 quart peeled pumpkin, cut into chunks

3 cups thickly sliced leeks or onions

3 carrots, cut into chunks

3 stalks celery, cut into large chunks

2 quarts water

1 teaspoon salt or salt substitute

1/2 teaspoon freshly ground pepper

2 tablespoons toasted sesame seeds

1 tablespoon caraway seeds

2 tablespoons chopped fresh tarragon or 1/2 teaspoon dried tarragon

4 tablespoons Barlean's organic flax oil

- Place the sweet potatoes, pumpkin, leeks or onions, carrots, celery, water, salt, and pepper in a large kettle. Bring to a boil, then cover and simmer for 40 minutes. The soup will be lumpy.

- With a slotted spoon, remove and reserve half of the carrots and celery and some firmer potato chunks.

- Puree the remainder of the soup in a food mill or blender until smooth.

- Return to the kettle and add the sesame seeds, caraway seeds, tarragon, and the reserved vegetables. Stir in the flax oil and serve.

SERVES 8

Lentil Soup

1 tablespoon extra virgin olive oil
2 large onions, finely diced
4 cloves garlic, crushed or minced
2 green bell peppers, finely diced
10 cups vegetable stock
2 carrots, thinly sliced
1¹/2 cups lentils
¹/3 teaspoon dried thyme
liberal seasoning with freshly ground black pepper
¹/2 teaspoon salt or salt substitute
1 28-ounce can plum tomatoes in their juice, finely chopped
1 pound fresh spinach, stems removed and finely chopped, or
   10-ounce package frozen chopped spinach, thawed
4 tablespoons Barlean's organic flax oil

- Heat the olive oil in a large stock pot over medium heat. Add the onions, garlic, and bell peppers and sauté for 10 minutes.

- Add the remaining ingredients, except the spinach and flax oil, and bring to a boil. Reduce the heat and simmer, stirring occasionally, for 45 minutes or until the lentils are tender.

- Add the spinach and cook for 5 minutes, or until the spinach has wilted and become tender.

- Remove from heat and stir in the flax oil.

SERVES 6

Curried Red Lentil Soup

1$1/2$ cups red lentils
4 cups water
$1/2$ teaspoon salt or salt substitute
2 medium potatoes, diced
1 tablespoon extra virgin olive oil
1 medium onion, chopped
2 cloves garlic, minced
1 teaspoon turmeric
1 teaspoon ground cumin
1 teaspoon ground coriander
$1/2$ teaspoon cayenne
2 to 3 tablespoons Barlean's organic flax oil

- Place the lentils in a strainer and rinse with cold, running water.
- Combine the lentils, water, and salt in a large pot. Bring to a boil and cook, uncovered, for 20 minutes over medium heat, stirring occasionally.
- Add the potatoes and stir.
- In a small skillet, heat the olive oil. Add the onion, garlic, and spices. Sauté until the onion begins to get tender.
- Add the onion mixture to the soup and cook until the potatoes are tender, about 20 minutes.
- Remove from heat and stir in the flax oil.

SERVES 4

Black Bean Soup

This soup can be made up to 4 days ahead: simply pour it into an airtight container, refrigerate, and reheat to serving temperature.

2 teaspoons extra virgin olive oil
2 medium red onions, chopped
1 jalapeño pepper, minced
2 large cloves garlic, minced
1 teaspoon ground cumin
1/2 teaspoon chili powder
4 cups cooked black beans
2 cups water
2 tablespoons Barlean's organic flax oil
2 tablespoons sour cream or plain nonfat yogurt to top

- Heat the olive oil in a medium saucepan. Add the onions and jalapeño pepper. Sauté over moderate heat, stirring frequently, until the onions begin to brown, about 4 minutes.
- Stir in the garlic and reduce the heat to low. Cook, stirring constantly, for 1 minute. Stir in the cumin and chili powder.
- Combine the onion mixture, beans, and water in a heavy pot. Cook over low heat, stirring occasionally, until the beans are hot, about 5 minutes.
- If a smooth texture is preferred, transfer the soup to a food processor or blender and puree until smooth.
- Once the soup is removed from heat, stir in the flax oil.
- Top with a dollop of sour cream or yogurt.

SERVES 4

Ratatouille Soup

1 pound tomatoes, chopped
1 onion, chopped
1 green bell pepper, chopped
2 cloves garlic, minced
2 bay leaves
tomato juice or water if necessary
1 eggplant, unpeeled and chopped
1 teaspoon dried basil
1 teaspoon dried marjoram
1/2 teaspoon dried oregano
1/2 teaspoon dried rosemary
1/4 cup chopped fresh parsley
3 tablespoons Barlean's organic flax oil

- In a soup pot, cook the tomatoes, onion, bell pepper, garlic, and bay leaves until almost tender. If the mixture is too thick, add tomato juice or water.
- Add the eggplant, basil, marjoram, oregano, and rosemary. Cook until the eggplant and other ingredients are tender.
- Add the parsley and heat through.
- Remove from heat and stir in the flax oil.
- Remove the bay leaves before serving. Serve hot or cold.

SERVES 4

Split Green Pea Soup

10 cups vegetable stock or water
2 cups split green peas, rinsed and drained
1 tablespoon extra virgin olive oil
1 large onion, finely chopped
1 stalk celery, finely chopped
1 large carrot, finely chopped
salt or salt substitute to taste
freshly ground black pepper to taste
3 tablespoons Barlean's organic flax oil

- In a large stock pot, bring the stock or water to a boil. Add the split peas. Cover and simmer over low heat for about 30 minutes.
- In a pan, heat the olive oil and add the onion, celery, and carrot. Cover and cook until the vegetables have softened, about 15 minutes.
- Add the softened vegetables to the split peas. Season with salt and pepper. Cover and simmer gently for 45 to 60 minutes, stirring occasionally to prevent the soup from sticking to the pot.
- Transfer to a blender. Add the flax oil and puree. If the soup seems too thick, add more water.

SERVES 6

Split Pea Soup
A warming and nourishing soup.

5 1/2 cups water
1 1/2 cups split peas, rinsed and drained
1 tablespoon concentrated vegetable stock or 1 vegetable bouillon cube
1/2 tablespoon onion powder
1/2 teaspoon dried dill weed or 1 tablespoon minced fresh dill
dash of cayenne
1/2 cup chopped green bell pepper
1/2 cup minced carrot
1/2 cup quartered and thinly sliced carrot
3 tablespoons Barlean's organic flax oil

- Bring the water to a boil in a large pot. Stir in the peas with the vegetable stock or bouillon cube. Cover and cook over low heat for 1 hour.
- Add the remaining spices and vegetables. Cover and simmer for 20 to 25 minutes.
- Remove from heat and cool to serving temperature.
- Stir in the flax oil and serve.

SERVES 6

6

ℰntrées and Vegetable Dishes

THE NO, NO-FAT "WEIGH" TO WEIGHT LOSS
AND MAINTENANCE

FLAX FOR THOUGHT Entrées are the focal point of our dining experience. We have grown to expect hearty, filling, and satisfying entrées, and so they should be. However, we have also been taught that fat is bad and that fat should be low or nonexistent in our main meals. We know from the introductory chapter to this book that this is really only half the story. Fat in meals causes a sensation of fullness and satisfaction. This

feeling of satisfaction and fullness effectively curtails our appetite and stabilizes our blood sugar and energy levels for longer periods compared with meals free of fat.

With the recipes presented in *Flax for Life!* you can experience the best of both worlds by limiting your intake of saturated fats and hydrogenated oils and by including the healing and protective essential fats found in flax oil. Flax oil added to your main meals will bring you the satisfaction you expect without the guilt associated with meals high in fat. The essential fatty acids in flax oil help to activate special fat-burning cells in your body that will, in turn, mobilize and burn the bad fats in your body tissues. Can we eat filling, satisfying meals and still maintain or even reduce our waistline? You bet we can, and the answer is the addition of the essential fatty acids found in flax oil.

Here are a few tips regarding entrées and vegetable dishes.

- Create ways to include flax oil in your entrées. Think of flax oil as a tasty carrier for other herbs and as a natural pick-me-up.
- Flax oil can be used as a delicious sauce over brown rice or freshly steamed vegetables.
- Remember, it is important to add flax oil after the cooking process in order to limit the oil's exposure to heat.

Angel Hair Pasta with Fresh Tomato Sauce

8 ounces angel hair pasta
3 large beefsteak tomatoes, cut into 1/2-inch cubes
1 large clove garlic, crushed
1/4 cup chopped fresh basil or 2 teaspoons dried basil
1/4 teaspoon salt or salt substitute
freshly ground black pepper to taste
2 tablespoons Barlean's organic flax oil

- Prepare the pasta according to directions on package.
- Combine the tomatoes, garlic, basil, salt, and pepper. Add the flax oil and whisk well.
- Add half of the sauce to the hot pasta and mix.
- Top with the remaining sauce.

SERVES 4

Winter Pesto

The perfect compliment to pasta dishes.

3 cups (tightly packed) fresh spinach leaves, rinsed and dried
1 tablespoon dried basil
4 cloves garlic
3 tablespoons extra virgin olive oil
2 tablespoons Barlean's organic flax oil
1/3 cup pine nuts
dash of salt or salt substitute

- Combine all ingredients in a blender or food processor and process until smooth.
- Refrigerate in a tightly sealed container until ready to use.
- Bring the pesto to room temperature before serving.

SERVES 6

Spaghetti with Marinara Sauce

3/4 pound spaghetti

1 tablespoon extra virgin olive oil

3/4 cup chopped onion

1/3 cup chopped celery

1/3 cup chopped carrot

1 medium clove garlic, crushed

1 tablespoon nutritional yeast (optional)

6 large tomatoes, peeled and chopped, or 28-ounce can peeled Italian tomatoes, drained and chopped

1/4 teaspoon dried oregano

1/4 teaspoon dried basil

pinch of salt or salt substitute to taste

freshly ground black pepper to taste

1 tablespoon tomato paste (optional)

1 tablespoon Barlean's organic flax oil

- Prepare the spaghetti according to directions on package.
- While the spaghetti cooks, prepare the sauce.
- Heat the olive oil in a medium pan. Add the onion, celery, carrot, and garlic. Sauté over medium heat for 3 minutes, stirring frequently. Add the yeast and stir well.
- Add the tomatoes, oregano, basil, salt, and pepper. Stir in the tomato paste. Cover and simmer over low heat, stirring occasionally, until the sauce becomes fairly uniform in consistency, about 20 minutes.
- Remove from heat and stir in the flax oil.
- Pour the sauce over the hot spaghetti.

SERVES 3

Vermicelli Pesto and Green Peas
A simple and delicious meal complimented with fresh basil.

1/2 pound vermicelli
2 cloves garlic, crushed
4 cups fresh basil leaves
4 tablespoons pine nuts
pinch of salt
1/4 cup Barlean's organic flax oil
1/4 cup extra virgin olive oil
2 cups green peas

- Prepare the pasta according to directions on package.
- While the pasta cooks, prepare the pesto.
- In a food processor or blender, combine the garlic, basil leaves, pine nuts, salt, flax and olive oils and process to a thick paste.
- Place the peas in a steamer and steam for 4 to 5 minutes or until tender.
- Remove 1/2 cup of the pasta water from pot before draining the pasta. Combine the pasta water with 1/4 cup of the pesto and stir well. (Store the remaining pesto.*)
- Place the pasta in a large bowl. Add the peas and pour the pesto over the top. Toss well.

* Note: Cover the remaining pesto with a thin layer of olive oil to prevent the basil leaves from turning brown. Refrigerate. Will keep for several weeks.

SERVES 2

Peanut Butter, Flax, and Carrot Sandwich
Packed with punch for a high-energy lunch.

1 tablespoon Barlean's organic flax oil
2 tablespoons natural peanut butter
2 slices whole-grain bread
1/4 cup shredded baby carrots
lettuce or alfalfa sprouts

- Combine the flax oil and peanut butter. Stir to an even consistency.
- Spread both pieces of bread with the flax–peanut butter mixture. Add the carrots and lettuce or sprouts.
- Eat!

SERVES 1

Whipped Acorn Squash and Yams
A twist on tradition by adding flax oil.

2 large acorn squash, halved
2 large or 4 medium yams
1/2 cup fresh orange juice
1 tablespoon pure maple syrup
cinnamon
grated nutmeg
3 tablespoons Barlean's organic flax oil

- Bake the squash and yams for 45 minutes to 1 hour or until tender.
- Scoop out the squash from the skins and place in a large mixing bowl or food processor. Remove the yam flesh from the skins and add to the squash.
- Add the orange juice, maple syrup, spices, and flax oil. Whip or mash together.

SERVES 6

Corn on the Cob with Spicy Flax Sauce
A tastier and healthier alternative to butter for delicious corn on the cob.

$1/2$ teaspoon pressed garlic or $1/2$ teaspoon garlic powder
$1/4$ teaspoon ground cumin
$1/4$ teaspoon paprika
dash of cayenne
2 tablespoons Barlean's organic flax oil
6 ears corn (fresh or frozen)

- Combine the garlic and spices with the flax oil.
- Bring a large pot of water to a boil. Add the corn and return to a boil, then boil for 3 minutes.
- Remove the corn from the water and brush generously with the spicy flax sauce.

SERVES 6

Marinated Artichokes
This is a great dish to serve while entertaining.

2 artichokes, cooked
1/2 cup orange juice
1/8 cup Barlean's organic flax oil
2 tablespoons tarragon vinegar
2 tablespoons chopped shallot or scallions
1 tablespoon minced fresh parsley
1 1/2 teaspoons grated orange peel
1/2 teaspoon salt or salt substitute
pinch of each: tarragon, basil, and chervil
1/4 teaspoon dry mustard
1/4 teaspoon Worcestershire sauce

- Cut the artichokes in half from tip to stem. Remove and discard the choke and the small inner leaves.
- Combine the remaining ingredients in a food processor or blender and process to an even consistency.
- Place the artichokes in a shallow dish and spoon the marinade over them. Cover and refrigerate overnight, turning occasionally.
- Serve the artichokes with some of the marinade spooned over the top.

SERVES 2

Marinated Roasted Red Peppers

4 large red bell peppers
4 tablespoons Barlean's organic flax oil
2 cloves garlic, crushed or sliced into thin slivers
1/2 teaspoon kelp powder or vegetable seasoning

- Place the peppers on a baking sheet in a preheated 400°F oven. Turn frequently until skin blisters on all sides.
- Remove the peppers from the oven and place in a paper bag. Close tightly. Allow to sit for 20 minutes while the skins sweat off.
- Peel the loose skins from the peppers, remove the seeds and ribs, and discard. Cut the peppers in strips of desired thickness.
- Combine the flax oil, garlic, and kelp powder in a medium bowl.
- Add the pepper strips and marinate at least 1 hour before using, or store in the refrigerator in a tightly sealed container until ready to use.

SERVES 4

Barlean's Marinated Red Pepper Sandwich
Nutritious and delicious.

2 slices whole-grain bread, lightly toasted
mayonnaise or Flax-Almond Mayonnaise (page 22)
Dijon mustard
Marinated Roasted Red Peppers (page 72)
grated carrot
thinly sliced cucumber

- Spread the bread generously with mayonnaise and mustard.
- Add the remaining ingredients.

SERVES 1

Sauerkraut Hawaiian Style
Combines sulfer-rich cruciferous vegetables with fatty acid–rich flax oil.

8 ounces sauerkraut with liquid
8 ounces red cabbage
1/2 cup diced pineapple
1 cup diced tomatoes
1 teaspoon soy sauce or tamari
2 tablespoons Barlean's organic flax oil

- Combine the sauerkraut with liquid, cabbage, pineapple, and tomatoes in a saucepan. Simmer for 30 minutes.
- Remove from heat and stir in the soy sauce and flax oil.
- Serve hot or cold.

SERVES 2 TO 3

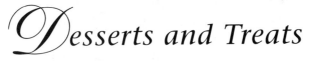
Desserts and Treats

FUN AND FROLIC WITH FLAX

FLAX FOR THOUGHT Desserts and treats are often considered the downfall of our dining experience. This belief is well founded because the majority of desserts and treats available to us are highly refined and full of refined sugar as well as unnatural saturated fats. How often have we heard "no dessert for me, I'm trying to drop a couple of pounds." An hour later, the well-intentioned diner is downing

a half gallon of ice cream from the carton. Is it possible to provide sensible, satisfying, and healthful desserts and treats for your friends, family, and self? Absolutely. And the result will be far healthier than a late-night binge.

As is common with other foods, much of the satisfaction that is found with desserts is because they bring satiety, the sense of fulfillment following a meal. The primary reason for satiety in foods is because of the fat found in them. If you've ever eaten a low-fat or no-fat dessert, you know what I mean. The sweetness might be there, but somehow you are left craving for more, so you have another and another and another—you get the idea. Not a bad way to sell more no-fat and low-fat desserts. Unfortunately, as we have learned, you end up eating more calories than if you had eaten just a sensible portion of a desert or treat that contained some fat—hopefully good fat.

The best news is that we can enjoy delicious, healthful, and satisfying desserts and treats without the guilt associated with highly refined or unhealthfully saturated and funny fat–laden desserts. You will find that by adding flax oil to desserts and treats, you can experience a sense of enjoyment and satisfaction with a single serving and avoid eating seconds and thirds. You will also appreciate the sustained energy and blood sugar levels that flax oil brings, satisfying your hunger for hours on end.

Here are a few suggestions for terrific flax desserts.

- With a little creativity, flax oil can be incorporated into many desserts. Try mixing flax oil half and half with pure maple syrup as a topping. Another option is to mix flax oil half and half with raw honey for a delicious, sweet spread or topping. Try pureeing the oil with your favorite berries in a blender or food processor.

- Spice up your flax oil with a dash of cinnamon, allspice, nutmeg, or other pleasant spice to make flax oil more applicable for use in desserts.

- In recipes that don't require excessive heating or baking, simply replace or reduce the less healthful oils in the recipe with flax oil. Because unrefined flax oil exerts a stronger flavor than refined oils, make sure the nutty flavor of quality flax oil will enhance the recipe.

Coconut-Mocha Cream Frosting

5 tablespoons whole wheat pastry flour
1 cup rice milk or soy milk
2 tablespoons Barlean's organic flax oil
1/4 teaspoon salt
2 teaspoons vanilla extract
3 tablespoons pure maple syrup
1/2 cup shredded coconut
1 teaspoon carob powder
1 teaspoon Pero, Roma, or other powdered coffee substitute

- In a small saucepan, combine the flour and milk. Bring to a boil, whisking constantly. If lumps appear, beat with an eggbeater until smooth. Stirring constantly, cook until the flour is thickened, about 2 minutes. Cool for 15 minutes.

- Place the flour mixture and the remaining ingredients in a blender and blend at medium speed until very smooth. Cool for 30 minutes. Whisk well before using.

FROSTS ONE SINGLE-LAYER CAKE

Carob–Peanut Butter Bars

1/2 cup carob powder
2/3 cup soy powder
2 tablespoons Barlean's organic flax oil
1/4 cup peanut butter
1/4 cup rice polishings
2 tablespoons brewers yeast, optional
2 tablespoons wheat germ
raw honey
chopped walnuts and almonds to top

- Place all ingredients in a bowl, adding enough honey to make a kneadable consistency.
- Spread in a square pan. Press the chopped nuts over the top. Chill.
- Cut into bars and serve.

MAKES 6 BARS

Flax, Bran, and Fruit Bars
A healthy snack alternative.

1/4 pound pitted dried prunes
1/4 pound dates
1/4 pound figs
1/4 pound raisins
1/4 cup raw honey
3 tablespoons lemon juice
3 tablespoons Barlean's organic flax oil
1 cup bran
1/2 cup wheat germ
1 tablespoon grated orange rind

- Process the fruit in a food processor.
- Combine the honey, lemon juice, flax oil, bran, wheat germ, and orange rind. Mix well.
- Combine the processed fruit with the other ingredients and mix well.
- Mold the mixture in a pan and refrigerate 1 hour.
- Cut into bars and serve.

MAKES 12 BARS

Tofu Yogurt

If you are allergic to milk or simply desire the nutritional benefits of soy, this is a great alternative to standard yogurt.

1/2 block silken tofu

1 to 1 1/2 cups frozen and chopped strawberries, blueberries, or raspberries

1 tablespoon Barlean's organic flax oil

1 teaspoon vanilla extract

1 teaspoon raw honey

- Combine ingredients in order listed in a food processor or blender and process to an even consistency.

SERVES 1

Peach Pie

1 standard whole wheat piecrust, baked to a light brown

5 to 6 large peaches, peeled

3 tablespoons fresh orange juice

1/2 cup raw cashew pieces

3 tablespoons pure maple syrup

1/2 cup water

1 teaspoon vanilla extract

1/2 cup Barlean's organic flax oil

fresh mint leaves for garnish

plain yogurt to top

- Slice the peaches into thin half moons.
- In a mixing bowl, combine the peaches with the orange juice and set aside.
- Place the cashews in a blender or food processor with the maple syrup, water, and vanilla. Process until creamy and smooth. While the blender is running on low speed, add the flax oil in a thin stream until the mixture thickens but is still slightly runny.
- Coat the bottom of the piecrust with a thin layer of the cashew mixture. Add a layer of peach slices in flower petal fashion, then spread with cashew mixture and continue layering, ending with a top layer of peaches. Garnish with mint leaves.
- Refrigerate for at least 2 hours before serving.
- Top with yogurt.

MAKES 1 PIE

Peach Melba

3 peaches, peeled and halved, or 6 canned peach halves (juice packed)
6 tablespoons vanilla or plain nonfat yogurt
1¹/₂ tablespoons Barlean's organic flax oil
6 tablespoons pureed raspberries

- Place the peach halves in individual sherbet glasses.
- Combine the yogurt and flax oil in a small bowl and stir thoroughly to homogenize.
- Top each peach with 1 tablespoon of the yogurt mixture and then with 1 tablespoon of the pureed raspberries.

SERVES 6

Sautéed Apples with Maple Syrup–Yogurt Topping
*A taste treat. This recipe is also good
with pears used in place of apples.*

6 medium apples, peeled and quartered
1 tablespoon butter
5 tablespoons pure maple syrup
¹/₄ teaspoon ground cloves
1¹/₂ teaspoons cinnamon
1 cup plain nonfat yogurt
4 tablespoons Barlean's organic flax oil
2 tablespoons chopped walnuts to top

- Cut each apple quarter into 4 slices.
- Sauté the apples in the butter for 5 minutes. Add 4 tablespoons of the maple syrup, the cloves, and one half of the cinnamon. Stir to coat the apples. Cook about 7 minutes more, until the apples are tender and the syrup thickens.
- Transfer to a medium bowl and chill for 1 hour.
- In another medium bowl, combine the yogurt, the remaining maple syrup and cinnamon, and the flax oil. Stir to an even consistency. Chill for at least 1 hour.
- When ready to serve, place the apple mixture in individual bowls. Spoon the yogurt mixture on top and sprinkle with the walnuts.

SERVES 6

Strawberry-Banana Pie

1 homemade or prepared whole wheat piecrust lightly browned in
  the oven

Strawberry Glaze

2 cups strawberries

2 tablespoons psyllium husks (available in health food stores)

2 tablespoons pure maple syrup

2 tablespoons Barlean's organic flax oil

Filling

3 medium bananas

3 cups strawberries

shredded coconut to top

- Blend the strawberries, psyllium, maple syrup, and flax oil. Pour
  two-thirds of the glaze into the crust, reserving one-third for the top.
- Thinly slice the bananas and strawberries. Cover the bottom of the
  pie first with a layer of half the strawberries, then with the banana
  slices. Top with a final layer of strawberries and the remainder of
  the glaze. Sprinkle with coconut.
- Refrigerate at least 3 hours before serving.

SERVES 6

Coconut, Carob, and Peanut Butter Balls

A taste treat better than See's candies. A favorite with kids!

1/2 cup natural peanut butter

1/2 cup Barlean's organic flax oil

1/2 cup shredded coconut (more if necessary)

1/4 cup carob powder

- In a bowl, combine the peanut butter and flax oil and mix
  thoroughly.
- Stir in the coconut and carob powder. If necessary, use additional
  coconut to thicken mixture.
- Form the dough into balls.
- Serve immediately, or cover and chill for future use.

Variations:

- add 1/4 cup raisins
- add 1/4 cup walnuts

SERVES 6

Spanish Baklava

*By using tortillas instead of filo dough we have come up
with a quick and easy south-of-the-border revision of the tasty
traditional Middle Eastern treat.*

1/2 cup water
1/4 cup raisins
2 flour or whole wheat tortillas
2 tablespoons Barlean's organic flax oil
1 tablespoon pure maple syrup
1 tablespoon raw honey
1/4 teaspoon cinnamon
1/2 cup plain yogurt
2 tablespoons crushed walnuts

- Heat the water to boiling. Add the raisins. Remove from heat and set aside.
- Heat the tortillas in a frying pan over low heat, maintaining softness and pliability (don't overcook).
- While heating the tortillas, combine the flax oil, maple syrup, honey, and cinnamon in a small bowl and whisk well.
- Pour the raisins into a strainer, discarding the water.
- Remove the tortillas from heat.
- Spread an even layer of the flax oil mixture over the entire face of both tortillas.
- Form a line with the yogurt across the center of the tortillas extending from edge to edge.
- Place the raisins and walnuts over the yogurt.
- Fold the tortillas on both ends and roll tightly (burrito style).
- With a sharp knife make several diagonal cuts in the rolled tortillas.
- Serve immediately, or chill for dessert.

SERVES 6

Flax Snacks

An excellent snack between meals. High in dietary fiber.

3/4 cup flax flour*

3 tablespoons oat flour

1 1/2 teaspoons cinnamon

1 1/2 teaspoons ground cloves

2 tablespoons peanut butter

1/2 cup rice syrup

coconut flakes (optional)

6 tablespoons ground almonds (optional)

* Grind whole flaxseed to the consistency of flour in a coffee grinder.

• Combine the flax flour, oat flour, cinnamon, and cloves in a mixing bowl. Add the peanut butter and rice syrup to the mixture. Knead thoroughly by hand.

• Tear pieces off and roll them between your hands into balls. You could also roll the mixture into a log, then cut the log into individual pieces.

• Place the coconut flakes and ground almonds on waxed paper. Press the rolled balls or pieces onto the coconut-almond mixture. (Optional)

• Serve immediately, or chill for future use.

MAKES ABOUT 2 DOZEN 1-INCH BALLS

Recipe submitted by Jo Ann Barlean

$\mathcal{F}$laxy Smoothies

FLAX YOUR MUSCLES
WITH SUPER SMOOTHIES

FLAX FOR THOUGHT Of all of the ways presented in *Flax for Life!* to incorporate essential fatty acids into a daily diet, I believe the addition of flax oil to smoothies (blender drinks) is one of the easiest and tastiest ways to get a daily dose of these vital nutrients. In addition, this method lends itself perfectly to the inclusion of a protein source as popularized by Dr. Johanna Budwig, a

Nobel Prize nominee, German biochemist, and the world's leading authority on fats and oils nutrition. Dr. Budwig contends that the combination of flax oil with a sulfur-rich protein, such as yogurt or cottage cheese, potentiates the power of the essential fatty acids in the flax oil. Since 1950, Dr. Budwig has treated cancer and other debilitating illnesses with this approach.

You will find these flaxy smoothies to be the perfect midday pick-me-up and, of course, an unbeatable drink after a workout.

Smoothie flax facts:

- Try a smoothie coupled with yogurt, fresh seasonal fruit, and flax oil for a breakfast on the run. You will be amazed at how long this formula will maintain your energy and blood sugar levels.

- Consider adding a scoop of your favorite protein powder or a dollop of yogurt to your smoothies in order to obtain the valuable oil/protein combination endorsed by Dr. Johanna Budwig. This is especially an effective method following a grueling workout. Bodybuilders and fitness buffs have popularized the use of flax oil in smoothies to help reduce the soreness and muscle fatigue associated with training. Mr. Jay Robb, a well-known author for bodybuilding magazines and a fat-burning expert, has coined the phrase "flax your muscles" as a testament to these truths.

- For those rare individuals who do not care for the rich taste of unrefined flax oil, the addition of the oil to smoothies goes virtually undetected.
- For those finicky kids, I do not know of a better way to sneak in the benefits of flax oil than through a delicious smoothie.
- Flax oil can be included in any existing smoothie recipe or in any recipe you could dream up.
- Smoothies—a terrific and delicious way to flax your way to good health!

Banana–Carob Chip Frosty
A chocolate-like treat.

2 medium frozen bananas
1 cup frozen rice milk or soy milk (use ice tray)
1 tablespoon peanut butter
1/4 cup carob chips
3/4 cup water
2 tablespoons Barlean's organic flax oil

- In a blender, combine ingredients in order listed and puree to a frosty consistency.

SERVES 2 TO 3

Strawberry and Cashew Nut Milk Smoothie
Rich, creamy, and nutritious too!

1 3/4 cups water
1/3 cup cashews
7 frozen strawberries
1/4 cup frozen blueberries
2 tablespoons Barlean's organic flax oil
2 tablespoons raw honey

- In a blender, combine ingredients in order listed and blend until rich and creamy.

SERVES 2

Pineapple and Cranberry Smoothie

1 cup chunk pineapple
1 medium banana
1 cup cranberry juice
1/2 cup plain nonfat yogurt
3 tablespoons raw honey
3 tablespoons Barlean's organic flax oil
2 cups ice (1 tray)

- In a blender, combine ingredients in order listed and puree to a smooth, frosty consistency.

SERVES 4

Pineapple and Date Smoothie

3/4 cup unsweetened pineapple juice
5 honey dates, pitted
1 frozen banana, sliced
2 tablespoons Barlean's organic flax oil
4 tablespoons plain nonfat yogurt (optional)
3 ice cubes

- In a blender, combine ingredients in order listed and blend until smooth.

SERVES 2

Very Cherry Smoothie

*Folkloric belief has established cherries as being beneficial
to people suffering from arthritis. The anti-inflammatory action of
essential fatty acid–rich flax oil serves to synergise their effect.*

2 cups pitted fresh cherries
1 cup plain nonfat yogurt
2 tablespoons Barlean's organic flax oil
1 tablespoon raw honey
1/4 teaspoon vanilla
1 cup ice (7 ice cubes)

- In a blender, combine ingredients in order listed and puree to a frosty consistency.

SERVES 2 TO 3

Pineapple-Strawberry Smoothie

1 1/2 cups chilled pineapple juice
2 tablespoons Barlean's organic flax oil
4 tablespoons nonfat yogurt (optional)
10 frozen strawberries
ice cubes

- In a blender, combine ingredients in order listed and puree to a smooth consistency, adding ice cubes as needed.

SERVES 2

Blueberry-Almond Smoothie
Refreshing, nourishing, and satisfying.

1 cup frozen blueberries
1 frozen banana
1/4 cup soft tofu (optional)
1/4 cup raw almonds
2 tablespoons Barlean's organic flax oil
2 tablespoons pure maple syrup
1 cup water or rice milk

- In a blender, combine ingredients in order listed and puree to a smooth consistency.

SERVES 2

Spicy Apple Smoothie
Rich in fiber and essential fatty acids.

2 apples, peeled
1 frozen banana
1/4 cup raisins, soaked
1/4 teaspoon peanut butter
2 tablespoons Barlean's organic flax oil
1 tablespoon raw honey
pinch of cinnamon
1 cup water
4 ice cubes

- In a blender, combine all ingredients and puree to a smooth consistency.

SERVES 2 TO 3

Carob Date Shake
A delectable, chocolatey-tasting, and protein-packed treat!

2/3 cup water
1 cup soft tofu
2/3 cup honey dates, pitted
1 frozen banana
1 cup crushed ice
2 tablespoons Barlean's organic flax oil
1 tablespoon roasted carob powder or cocoa powder
2 teaspoons Pero, Roma, or other powdered coffee substitute

- In a blender, combine ingredients in order listed. Blend on high speed to desired consistency.

SERVES 2

Nutty Buddy Peanut Butter Smoothie
A must for the peanut butter lover! A favorite with kids.

1 cup rice milk, soy milk, or nonfat milk
1 banana
2 tablespoons peanut butter
2 tablespoons raw honey
2 tablespoons plain nonfat yogurt (optional)
2 tablespoons Barlean's organic flax oil
2 tablespoons wheat germ
1/2 teaspoon vanilla
2 cups ice (1 tray)

- In a blender, combine ingredients in order listed and blend until smooth or to desired consistency.

SERVES 2

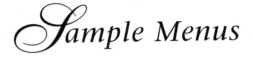

Sample Menus

The menus presented in this section may be used as presented or used completely independently of each other. Mix and match, but always keep in mind a balanced, nutritional diet.

DAY ONE

Breakfast
Barlean's Best Oatmeal. 14
2 slices Multigrain Bread 20
Plain or flavored yogurt

Lunch
Bean or meat tostadas
Fresh Mexican Salsa (to top tostadas). . 22
Gazpacho. 56

Snack
Flax, Bran, and Fruit Bars. 77

Dinner
Pasta of your choice
Winter Pesto (to top pasta) 68
Quick Bread (toasted with
    crushed garlic) 15
Caesar Salad. 43

Dessert
Tofu Yogurt 78

DAY TWO

Breakfast
Buttery Banana Pancakes. 12
Yogurt (to top pancakes)
Fresh fruit in season
Glass of regular, soy, or rice milk

Lunch
Tuna Salad Supreme. 39
Barley Vegetable Soup 57
Radishes and celery

Snack
Strawberry and Cashew Nut Milk
    Smoothie 84

Dinner
3 ounces canned or poached salmon
Pumpkin Seed–Mint Sauce (to top
    fish) 55
Tossed green salad
Cucumber-Dill Dressing. 31

Dessert
Peach Melba. 79

DAY THREE

Breakfast
Fruit Lupes. 10
2 slices Multigrain Bread 20
Glass of regular, soy, or rice milk

Lunch
Peanut Butter, Flax, and Carrot
    Sandwich 70
Baked tortilla chips

Snack
Very Cherry Smoothie 85

Dinner
4 ounces shrimp
Szechwan Peanut Sauce (to marinate
    shrimp). 54
Mixed greens salad
Green Goddess Taiwanese Style 30
Brown rice with soy sauce or tamari

Dessert
Strawberry-Banana Pie 80

DAY FOUR

Breakfast
Hot Carob Cereal 11
2 slices Multigrain Bread 20
Glass of regular, soy, or rice milk

Lunch
Brown Rice and Spinach Salad 38
Curried Red Lentil Soup 61
Whole-grain crackers

Snack
Coconut, Carob, and Peanut Butter
   Balls 80

Dinner
Angel Hair Pasta 68
Marinated Artichokes 72
Mixed vegetable salad
Herbal Bouquet Salad Dressing 32

Dessert
Sautéed Apples with Maple Syrup–
   Yogurt Topping 79

DAY FIVE

Breakfast
French Toast with Flax-Maple Syrup . . 13
Yogurt (to top French toast)
Fresh fruit in season
Glass of regular, soy, or rice milk

Lunch
Taco Salad 45
Black Bean Soup 62
Tortilla strips

Snack
Nutty Buddy Peanut Butter Smoothie . . 87

Dinner
4 ounces baked halibut
Mediterranean Salad 40
Oregano Dressing 31
Baked potato

Dessert
Peach Pie 78

DAY SIX

Breakfast
Fresh Fruit Breakfast Muesli 9
2 slices Wheat-Free Flax Bread 16
Glass of regular, soy, or rice milk

Lunch
Marinated Roasted Red Peppers 72
Barlean's Marinated Red Pepper
   Sandwich 73
Baked tortilla chips
Dill pickle

Snack
Banana–Carob Chip Frosty 84

Dinner
Spaghetti with Marinara Sauce 69
Whole-Grain Flax Bread (toasted with
   crushed garlic) 17
Caesar Salad 43

Dessert
Spanish Baklava 81

DAY SEVEN

Breakfast
Spanish Omelet
Southwestern Sauce (to top omelet) . . . 53
Quick Bread (toasted) 15
Barlean Butter (to top bread) 12

Lunch
Hummus 23
Pita bread (fill with hummus)
Braised vegetables
Eggplant Dip (for vegetables) 26

Snack
Blueberry-Almond Smoothie 86

Dinner
4 ounces broiled chicken
Mashed potatoes
Flax Gravy 51
Small green salad

Dessert
Carob–Peanut Butter Balls 77

Resources and Recommended Reading

RESOURCES

Barlean's Organic Oils
4936 Lake Terrell Road
Ferndale, WA 98248
(800) 445-3529

Barlean's is considered by many leading health authorities and lay persons alike as the manufacturer of choice for organic flaxseed and other vegetable oils. Barlean's has attracted and secured the endorsement of Dr. Johanna Budwig, Dr. Michael Murray, Miss Ann Louise Gittleman, and Dr. Robert Erdmann.

To locate the services of a naturopathic physician in your area write or call:
The American Association of Naturopathic Physicians
P.O. Box 20386
Seattle, WA 98102
(206) 323-7610

RECOMMENDED READING

Fats That Can Save Your Life
Author: Dr. Robert Erdmann

A complete and entertaining sourcebook outlining the power of the essential fatty acids found in flax and the dramatic and even lifesaving capabilities they possess.

Understanding Fats & Oils:
Your Guide to Healing with Essential Fatty Acids
Authors: Dr. Michael Murray, N.D., and Jade Beutler, R.R.T., R.C.P.

A brief, yet comprehensive, review of fats and oils biochemistry. In addition, the healing potential of flax oil on particular diseases is explored. Cancer, multiple sclerosis, and allergic conditions are addressed. All covered in a little over 100 pages! Other similar books take over 400 pages to cover these issues.

Flax Oil as a True Aid Against Arthritis, Heart Infarction, Cancer and Other Diseases
Author: Dr. Johanna Budwig

A comprehensive review of the groundbreaking research of the world's leading expert on fats and oils nutrition and flax oil, German biochemist and Nobel Prize nominee Dr. Johanna Budwig. An in-depth study of the full potential of flax in the human diet.

These three books are available through Barlean's Organic Oils by calling or writing:

> Barlean's Organic Oils
> 4936 Lake Terrell Road
> Ferndale, WA 98248
> (800) 445-3529

The revised *Beyond Pritikin*
Author: Ann Louise Gittleman

Chronicles Miss Gittleman's experience with the Pritikin longevity centers and her decision to employ essential fatty acids in her clinical practice. The new revision of the original 1988 edition contains all the latest information on the healing essential fatty acids. An extremely enjoyable read for anyone interested in health and essential fatty acids.

Available through Uni-Key by calling or writing:

> Uni-Key
> P.O. Box 7168
> Bozeman, Montana 59771
> (800) 888-4353

References

Adlercreutz, H., et al. 1986. Determination of urinary lignans and phytoestrogen metabolites, potential antiestrogens and anticarcinogens, in urine of women on various habitual diets. *J. Steroid Biochem.* 25:791–97.

Belch, J. F., et al. 1988. Effects of altering dietary essential fatty acids on requirements for non-steroidal anti-inflammatory drugs in patients with rheumatoid arthritis: A double blind placebo controlled study. *Ann. Rheum. Dis.* 47:96–104.

Benquet, C., et al. 1994. Modulation of exercise-induced immunosuppression by dietary polyunsaturated fatty acids in mice. *J. Toxicol. Environ. Health* 43:225–37.

Berry, E. M., and J. Hirsch. 1986. Does dietary linolenic acid influence blood pressure? *Am. J. Clin. Nutr.* 44:336–40.

Bierenbaum, M. L., et al. 1993. Reducing atherogenic risk in hyperlipemic humans with flax seed supplementation: A preliminary report. *J. Am. Coll. Nutr.* 12:501–4.

Bierenbaum, M. L., and T. R. Watkins. 1992. Improving atherogenic risk in hyperlipemic humans with flax seed supplementation. *Proc. 54th Annual Flax Institute of the U.S.*, 5–6.

Bjerve, K. S., et al. 1992. Clinical studies with alpha-linolenic acid and long chain n-3 fatty acids. *Nutrition* 8:130–32.

Booyens, J., and C. F. Van Der Merwe. 1992. Margarines and coronary artery disease. *Med. Hypothesis* 37:241–44.

Borkman, M., et al. 1993. The relationship between insulin sensitivity and the fatty acid composition of skeletal-muscle phospholipids. *New Engl. J. Med.* 328:238–44.

Bougnoix, P., et al. 1994. Alpha-linolenic acid content of adipose breast tissue: A host determinant of the risk of early metastasis in breast cancer. *Br. J. Cancer* 70:330–34.

Carter, J. F. 1993. Potential of flaxseed and flax oil in baked goods and other products in human nutrition. *Cereal Foods World* 38:753–59.

Chan, J. K., V. M. Bruce, and B. E. McDonald. 1991. Dietary-alpha-linolenic acid is as effective as oleic acid and linoleic acid in lowering blood cholesterol in normolipidemic men. *Am. J. Clin. Nutr.* 53:1230–34.

Cobias, L., et al. 1991. Lipid, lipoprotein, and hemostatic effects of fish vs. fishoil w-3 fatty acids in mildly hyperlipidemic males. *Am. J. Clin. Nutr.* 53:1210–16.

Cunnane, S. C., ed. 1991. Symposium proceedings: Third Toronto essential fatty acid workshop on alpha-linolenic acid in human nutrition and disease. May 17–18, 1991, University of Toronto, Toronto, Ontario, Canada. *Nutrition* 7:435–46.

Cunnane, S. C., et al. 1990. Potential uses of flax in human nutrition. *Proc. 53rd Annual Flax Institute of the U.S.*, 1–7.

Cunnane, S. C., et al. 1991. Alpha-linolenic acid in humans: Direct functional role or dietary precursor. *Nutrition* 7:437–39.

de Lorgeril, M., et al. 1994. Mediterranean alpha-linolenic acid-rich diet in secondary prevention of coronary heart disease. *Lancet* 343:1454–59.

Dieken, H. 1992. Use of flaxseed as a source of omega-3 fatty acids in humans. *Proc. 54th Annual Flax Institute of the U.S.*, 1–5.

Hollstun, J. L. 1994. Survey results regarding increased utilization of flaxseed in the U.S. baking industry. *Proc. 55th Annual Flax Institute of the U.S.*, 98–101.

Kagawa, Y., et al. 1982. Eicosapolyenoic acids of serum lipids of Japanese Islanders with low incidence of cardiovascular diseases. *J. Nutr. Sci. Vitaminol.* 28:441–53.

Kelley, D. S. 1992. Alpha-linolenic acid and immune response. *Nutrition* 8:215–17.

Kremer, J., et al. 1985. Effects of manipulation of dietary fatty acids on clinical manifestation of rheumatoid arthritis. *Lancet* (January 26):184–87.

Lampe, J. W., et al. 1994. Urinary lignan and isoflavonoid excretion in premenopausal women consuming flaxseed powder. *Am. J. Clin. Nutr.* 60:122–28.

Longnecker, M. P. 1993. Do trans fatty acids in margarine and other foods increase the risk of coronary heart disease? *Epidemiology* 4:492–95.

Magaro, M., et al. 1988. Influence of diet with different lipid composition on neutrophil composition on neutrophil chemiluminescence and disease activity in patients with rheumatoid arthritis. *Ann. Rheum. Dis.* 47:793–96.

Mantzioris, E., et al. 1994. Dietary substitution with alpha-linolenic acid-rich vegetable oil increases eicosapentaenoic acid concentrations in tissues. *Am. J. Clin. Nutr.* 59:1304–9.

Mazen, H., et al. 1992. Nutritional aspects of flaxseed in the human diet. *Proc. 54th Annual Flax Institute of the U.S.*, 48–53.

Mensink, R. P., and M. B. Katan. 1990. Effect of dietary trans fatty acids on high-density and low-density lipoprotein cholesterol levels in healthy subjects. *New Engl. J. Med.* 323:439–45.

Nettleton, J. A. 1991. Omega-3 fatty acids: Comparison of plant and seafood sources in human nutrition. *J. Am. Diet. Assoc.* 91:331–37.

Nielsen, G. L., et al. 1992. The effects of dietary supplementation with n-3 polyunsaturated fatty acids in patients with rheumatoid arthritis: A randomized, double-blind trial. *Eur. J. Clin. Invest.* 22:687–91.

Ornish, D., et al. 1990. Can lifestyle changes reverse coronary heart disease? *Lancet* 336:129–33.

Pelikanova, T., et al. 1989. Insulin secretion and insulin action are related to the serum phospholipid fatty acid pattern in healthy men. *Metab. Clin. Exp.* 38:188–92.

Ratnayake, W. A. 1992. Flaxseed: Chemical stability and nutritional properties. *Proc. 54th Annual Flax Institute of the U.S.*, 37–47.

Rose, D. P., and M. A. Hatala. 1994. Dietary fatty acids and breast cancer invasion and metastasis. *Nutr. Cancer* 21:103–11.

Sandker, G. N., et al. 1993. Serum cholesterol ester fatty acids and their relation with serum lipids in elderly men in Crete and the Netherlands. *Eur. J. Clin. Nutr.* 47:201–8.

Sardesai, V. M. 1992. The essential fatty acids. *Nutr. Clin. Practice* (August):179–86.

Schlomo, Y., and R. L. Carasso. 1993. Modulation of learning, pain thresholds, and thermoregulation in the rat by preparations of free purified alpha-linolenic and linoleic acids: Determination of the optimal w3-to-w6 ratio. *Proc. Natl. Acad. Sci.* 90:10345–47.

Schmidt, E. B., and J. Dyerberg. 1994. Omega-3 fatty acids: Current status in cardiovascular medicine. *Drugs* 47:405–24.

Seidelin, K. N., B. Myrup, and B. Fischer-Hansen. 1992. n-3 fatty acids in adipose tissue and coronary artery disease are inversely correlated. *Am. J. Clin. Nutr.* 55:1117–19.

Serraino, M., and L. U. Thompson. 1991. The effect of flaxseed supplementation on early risk markers for mammary carcinogenesis. *Cancer Letters* 60:135–42.

Serraino, M., and L. U. Thompson. 1992. The effect of flaxseed supplementation on the initiation and promotional stages of mammary tumorigenesis. *Nutr. Cancer* 17:153–59.

Serraino, M., and L. U. Thompson. 1992. Flaxseed supplementation and early markers of colon carcinogenesis. *Cancer Letters* 63:159–65.

Serraino, M., et al. 1992. Effects of long term flaxseed supplementation on carcinogen and non-carcinogen treated rats. *Proc. 54th Annual Flax Institute of the U.S.,* 32–36.

Setchell, K. D. R., and H. Adlercreutz. 1988. Mammalian lignans and phytoestrogens: Recent studies on their formation, metabolism, and biological role in health and disease. In *Role of gut flora in toxicology and cancer,* ed. I. R. Rowland, 315–43. London: Academic Press.

Simopoulos, A. P. 1991. Omega-3 fatty acids in health and disease and in growth and development. *Am. J. Clin. Nutr.* 54:438–63.

Singer, P. 1992. Alpha-linolenic acid vs. long-chain fatty acids in hypertension and hyperlipidemia. *Nutrition* 8:133–35.

Stitt, P. 1988. Efficacy of feeding flax to humans and other animals. *Proc. 52nd Annual Flax Institute of the U.S.,* 37–40.

Stitt, P. 1988. Factors in flaxseed that help prevent cancer. *Proc. 52nd Annual Flax Institute of the U.S.,* 40–42.

Swank, R. L. 1991. Multiple sclerosis: Fat-oil relationship. *Nutrition* 7:368–76.

Thompson, L. U. 1987. *Effect of flaxseed on breast and colon cancer: A short term study.* Flax Council of Canada, 3–42.

Thompson, L. U., et al. 1991. Mammalian lignan production from various foods. *Nutr. Cancer* 16:43–52.

Willett, W. C., et al. 1993. Intake of trans fatty acids and risk of coronary heart disease among women. *Lancet* 341:581–85.

Zimmermann, D. C. 1988. Flax, linseed oil and human nutrition. *Proc. 52nd Annual Flax Institute of the U.S.,* 30–36.

ABOUT THE AUTHOR

Jade Beutler is a professional, licensed health care practitioner. He holds the dual credentials of R.C.P. and R.R.T. His clinical experience in adult and neonatal intensive care, pediatrics, and emergency medicine spans over 10 years. Mr. Beutler has been recognized by America's largest health maintenance organization as one of the top professionals in his field. He has been featured in the *San Diego Union*, the *Los Angeles Times*, and numerous trade journals. In addition, as a result of his passion for alternative, natural methods to treat degenerative disease, he serves as a consultant to the nutrition industry. Jade maintains a position on the Advisory Board of his alma mater California College for Health Sciences.